FIDEL CASTRO

IN HIS OWN WORDS

ALEX MOORE

Racehorse Publishing

Racehorse Publishing books may be purchased in bulk at special discounts for sales promotion, corporate gifts, fund-raising, or educational purposes. Special editions can also be created to specifications. For details, contact the Special Sales Department, Skyhorse Publishing, 307 West 36th Street, 11th Floor, New York, NY 10018 or info@skyhorsepublishing.com.

Racehorse Publishing™ is a pending trademark of Skyhorse Publishing, Inc.®,a Delaware corporation.

Visit our website at www.skyhorsepublishing.com.

10 9 8 7 6 5 4 3 2 1

Library of Congress Cataloging-in-Publication Data is available on file.

Cover design by Michael Short

Cover and insert photographs: Shutterstock

Print ISBN: 978-1-63158-190-8

Ebook ISBN: 978-1-63158-191-5

Printed in the United States of America

TABLE OF CONTENTS

Introduction..1

Chapter One: Castro the Bold Young Boy.....................4

Chapter Two: Learning to Rebel.................................10

Chapter Three: The Student Rebel..............................17

Chapter Four: Castro and Chibas................................23

Chapter Five: Castro vs. Batista.................................28

Chapter Six: Planning Moncada Barracks Attack............33

Chapter Seven: Absolved by History...........................38

Chapter Eight: Imprisoned.......................................44

Chapter Nine: Personal Upheaval...............................49

Chapter Ten: Training an Army in Mexico....................54

Chapter Eleven: Castro and Che.................................59

Chapter Twelve: The Granma Landing.........................64

Chapter Thirteen: The Takedown...............................68

Chapter Fourteen: Batista Falls.................................73

Chapter Fifteen: Changing the Government..................78

Chapter Sixteen: Military Tribunals............................83

Chapter Seventeen: Religion, Race, & Revolution............87

Chapter Eighteen: Castro's Social Reform.........................92

Chapter Nineteen: Castro and Women's Reform...............97

Chapter Twenty: Castro Meets World...........................101

Chapter Twenty-One: Castro and Khrushchev..............106

Chapter Twenty-Two: Trouble in Playa Girón
    (the Bay of Pigs)...110

Chapter Twenty-Three: Cuban Missile Crisis...............116

Chapter Twenty-Four: Castro and Kennedy...................121

Chapter Twenty-Five: Reaching Out
    to Latin America and Beyond.............................125

Chapter Twenty-Six: Castro and the Fall
    of the USSR...130

Chapter Twenty-Seven: Emigration Issues.....................134

Chapter Twenty-Eight: Castro in Africa.......................139

Chapter Twenty-Nine: Cuban Economics 143

Chapter Thirty: Castro and Nelson Mandela...........................147

Chapter Thirty-One: Castro and Chávez....................151

Chapter Thirty-Two: Mending Fences............................157

Chapter Thirty-Three: Health
    and Consequences...162

Chapter Thirty-Four: Stepping Down.....................166

Chapter Thirty-Five: Castro's Retirement................168

Chapter Thirty-Six: The Castros and Obama............171

Chapter Thirty-Seven: The Final Farewell....................175

Chapter Thirty-Eight: Cuba
       and the U.S.: A Shaky Future...................................178

Excerpts from Castro's Speeches.....................................185

      History Will Absolve Me....................................186

      To The U.N. General Assembly: The Problem
      of Cuba and Its Revolutionary Policy................205

      May Day Celebration: Cuba
      Is A Socialist Nation...212

Bibliography...220

INTRODUCTION

It's difficult to imagine a more polarizing figure in the 20th and early 21st centuries than Fidel Castro. In reading and researching his life and political rise and growth, I have been able to find nearly as many evaluations, books, and articles that praise him as a hero as there are that proclaim he's the devil himself.

Which is the true Fidel?

I've come to the conclusion that really depends—and probably always will—on perception.

On the one hand, Fidel was a hero. Since taking the reins in Cuba, he improved conditions for women and minorities and increased literacy, among other progressive advances. He helped in the fight against apartheid. He was revered by some world leaders, including Nelson Mandela, as a tireless humanitarian.

On the other hand, he nationalized businesses, cut into profit margins, and socialized health care—which, from wherever you stand, is good or bad. He was reviled by some world leaders, including any American Republican president who's been in office since the Cuban Revolution in 1959.

Did he exile the wealthy? Throw them out of the country and take away their land and homes? It depends on whom you ask. Some will angrily stand true to this conviction until their dying breath; others will say this wasn't the case, that the wealthy ran to the U.S., where they waited in vain for the U.S. government to oust the cunning Communist.

From whichever side of the Fidel fence you sit, what remains undeniable is that Fidel Castro was a powerful man with powerful ideas, who devised a revolution and maintained control of a country for more than five decades.

The illegitimate son of a wealthy landowner and the cook from the house that landowner had shared with his first family and wife, Fidel didn't grow up in poverty himself, but it surrounded him. Many kids from around the area would never finish high school, let alone grade school, because their families had no money. Fidel studied away from home with the Jesuits, and went on to complete college and law school. Not much for classroom learning, he read everything from literature to law and public policy, and developed a deep, abiding passion for Marxism, which changed his life.

He got involved in politics while still a student, and after graduating and setting up his own law practice, he began organizing and plotting against Fulgencio Batista, who had taken control of Cuba in a military coup. His first attempt failed; in training for his second attempt, he solidified an enduring friendship with Argentine revolutionary Ernesto "Che" Guevara, and together with Fidel's brother, Raul, they took back Cuba.

In power, Fidel did things that were objectionable, like abolish the multiple-party system and elections in general, nationalize business, and socialize reforms. He became an enemy to capitalists everywhere, even inspiring the United

States to attack Cuba (with Cuban exiles, incidentally) in the early 1960s. In making "friends" with a Communist super-power, he nearly had the power to end the world, or so was the perception during the Cuban Missile Crisis.

While the economy of Cuba has ebbed and flowed—in large part due to the embargo imposed by the United States and the fall of the USSR—he remained at the helm for more than five decades. Love him or hate him, one can't deny the impact had on the world for a half century.

The primary focus of this book is to create a profile of Fidel Castro by "painting" with his own words. In other words, what comes through here is the history of Fidel, according to Fidel. History at large may be able to pinpoint the irony and the untruths in his words, but there's no denying the clarity, the focus, the conviction, and the passion of his thoughts.

"History will absolve me," said Fidel in his famous speech, defending himself, during his trial for the attack on the Moncada Barracks. Whether that will be true in everyone's interpretation of history, of course, remains to be seen.

—Alex Moore
October 2013

CHAPTER ONE

CASTRO THE BOLD YOUNG BOY

November 6, 1940
Santiago de Cuba
Mr. Franklin Roosevelt, President of the United States.

My good friend Roosevelt I don't know very English, but I know as much as write to you. I like to hear the radio, and I am very happy, because I heard in it, that you will be President for a new (periodo). I am twelve years old. I am a boy but I think very much but I do not think that I am writing to the President of the United States. If you like, give me a ten dollars bill green american, in the letter, because never, I have not seen a ten dollars bill green american and I would like to have one of them.

My address is:

Sr Fidel Castro
Colegio de Dolores
Santiago de Cuba
Oriente Cuba

I don't know very English but I know very much Spanish and I suppose you don't know very Spanish but you know very English because you are American but I am not American.

(Thank you very much)
Good by. Your friend,
(Signed)
Fidel Castro

If you want iron to make your sheaps ships I will show to you the bigest (minas) of iron of the land. They are in Mayari Oriente Cuba.

Fidel Castro was the third of his mother's seven children, born on Aug. 13, 1926, on their farm in Birán, Cuba. His parents kept busy running the large family farm and bearing and raising his younger siblings. As a result, much of his young life was spent at boarding schools where his parents paid others to look after him. Fidel's formal education began at the young age of four at the country school in Birán. His older brother and sister, Ramón and Angelita, attended the school, and were instructed by a teacher who lived in Santiago and who would come to Birán to teach lessons and stay at the schoolhouse. Although he was only four, Fidel would join his older brother and sister when they went to school, and they gave him a desk right up front. Two years later, when Fidel was six, his parents sent his sister Angelita to Santiago to live and study with their teacher, and young Fidel went along. Soon after, their brother Ramón came too, and all three children lived as boarders with the teacher's family.

Fidel hated living with the teacher in Santiago. Her family was poor, and Fidel's life of freedom and plenty in Birán did not prepare him for the dirty, crowded, restrictive conditions in the small city. Fidel wasn't sent to school or given lessons, and spent his time idly about the house, or playing in the street with other young boys. And he was always hungry. In Birán there was always enough to eat, but at the teacher's house the meals were divided between the whole family. Fidel explained in a later interview:

> "Suddenly I discovered that rice was very tasty, and sometimes they'd serve the rice with a piece of sweet potato, or some picadillo—I don't remember that there was ever any bread—but the problem was that the same little bit of food, for six or seven people, was supposed to last through lunch and dinner—the food that was sent in at lunch. The food came from the house of one of the teacher's cousins, whom they called Cosita, 'Little Bit' or 'Little Thing'. She was a very fat lady. I don't know why they called her Cosita. Apparently, she was the one who ate all the food."

Fidel and his siblings were delivered from this living situation one day when Lina arrived to visit her three eldest and found them remarkably malnourished. She brought them to a café to eat their fill of ice cream and mangoes, and then brought them back home to the farm in Birán.

The next time the teacher returned to the little town, Fidel and his brother made a plan to get revenge. The two set up a fort of logs across from the schoolhouse and, using a slingshot, fired stones up and onto the galvanized zinc roof, making a huge racket. Fidel recalled the prank with pride. "The rocks landing on that zinc roof . . . by the time two or three were hitting the roof, there'd be two or three more in the air—we considered ourselves experts at that." This was Fidel's first real act of rebellion, a childish act of revenge against an authority who he'd perceived mistreated him.

As he continued with his schooling, he found plenty of other opportunities to raise his voice—and his fists.

After leaving the teacher's house, Fidel returned to Santiago to study at the Colegio de La Salle from the first through the fifth grades, boarding at the school's facilities and sharing a room with his brothers and a friend. Here there was plenty to eat, and Fidel enjoyed living at the school, especially when they would visit the facilities by the water, where he could swim and fish and play sports with the other boys.

It wasn't long before Fidel clashed with his teachers. He fought with one in particular, Vice Principal Brother Bernardo, who was in charge of boarding students. Fidel had made a particular enemy of this vice principal, he said, by fighting with another student who happened to be one of Brother Bernardo's favorites. The vice principal slapped him for this, hard. Later he slapped Fidel again, for speaking out of turn while waiting in line.

The third and final time he raised his hand to Fidel was in the courtyard, while boys were getting ready to play a game. Fidel was scrabbling with his classmates, deciding who would be at bat first, when he felt the vice principal hit him on the side of the head.

> *"But that was the last time, because I just blew up. I was so furious that I took those buttered rolls [from breakfast] and threw them right in the vice principal's face, as hard as I could, and then I ran at him and jumped on him like a little tiger—biting him, kicking him, hitting him with my fists, in front of the whole school. That was my second rebellion. I was a student and he was a figure of authority who abused and humiliated a student."*

Needless to say, Fidel and his brothers soon left the Colegio de La Salle and were sent home again to the farm in Birán. As punishment for their bad behavior, the boys' parents decided they would not be sent to another school. This suited Fidel's brothers, but Fidel was angry. This was clearly another instance where his opinions and those of the authority figures clashed—and so Fidel rebelled again, this time threatening to burn his house down if his parents didn't send him to school. Fidel claimed his parents were impressed with his enthusiasm for learning, or, as Fidel put it, "My mother was always the peacemaker. My father, very understanding—he may have liked how firm I was in defending my right to go to school. Whatever the case, my parents decided to send me off to school again." It is notable that in this retelling, Castro said he was *defending his right*; he frames his threat as an instance of standing against an authority to defend what is right, where another observer might say he was demanding he get his own way, and by threatening violence, no less. Even from a young age, Fidel Castro was a man unafraid to ask for what he wanted.

As a result of Fidel's successful campaign to be sent back

to school, he was soon enrolled at the Jesuit-run Colegio de Dolores in Santiago. Here, Fidel got along with his teachers. The Jesuits, it seems, knew what to do with a spirited young boy. Fidel said of them later, "They know how to form boys' characters. If you do risky, difficult things, engage in that sort of activities, they see that as proof of an enterprising, determined character—a 'get-up-and-go' sort of character. They don't discourage it." As a Jesuit school well known for its high educational standards, the Colegio de Dolores was a popular school for wealthy students like Fidel. It was here that Fidel began to learn English, and penned his letter to President Franklin Delano Roosevelt. He spoke of the letter casually many years after the fact, explaining that he wrote it while they were learning English from a textbook. "After the triumph of the Revolution, the Americans found my letter and published it, thanks to which I have a copy of it, because I didn't keep one. And there are people who've told me that if Roosevelt had only sent me $10, I wouldn't have given the United States so many headaches!" Castro didn't offer much other information about this strange moment in time, although he did say he got a response and that they hung a copy on the bulletin board. But the letter gives an interesting view of a young man who had learned to speak up early in life, and who was unafraid of directly addressing authority.

CHAPTER TWO

LEARNING TO REBEL

"I was the son of a landowner, not the grandson. If I'd been the grandson of a rich family I'd have been born . . . I'd have an aristocratic birth, and all my friends and all my culture would have been marked by a sense of superiority over other people. But in fact, where I was born, everybody was poor . . . My own family, on my mother's side, was poor . . . and my father's family in Galicia was also very poor."

When one thinks of Fidel Castro rising up to overthrow the "tyranny of capitalism," one might imagine that he grew up at the butt end of the economic system, that it crushed his family and his young spirit enough that rebelling against it was all he could do. However, it's interesting to note that Fidel Castro did not grow up in poverty, or anything close to it. Yet the concept of the injustice of poverty, coupled with an innate rebellious streak, were what would eventually propel Fidel to act against a system that had some having more at the expense of others.

Fidel had a rebellious streak, and one could surmise it

was in his blood. Fidel's father, Ángel Castro, hadn't always necessarily played by the rules himself. The elder Castro hailed from Galicia, Spain. In 1895, at aget 17, he signed up with the Spanish Colonial Army, apparently paid by a wealthy landowner to take the landowner's place in the Army.

Nearing the end of the 19th century, Spain's once-vast stake in North America had dwindled down to Puerto Rico and Cuba. While the Cuban Independence Movement began in the 1880s, it was not until around the point that Ángel had joined the Spanish Army that the movement was beginning to be taken seriously by Spain, and 7,000 soldiers were sent to Cuba to "look after" Spain's interests on the small island, Ángel among them.

But the once-thriving world power of Spain was in a shaky place in the late 1890s, and when Spanish Prime Minister Canavas del Castillo was assassinated in 1897, the resulting confusion and unrest in the Spanish government gave the insurgents the open window they needed to take control of Cuba, and, with the help of America, were finally able to push out Spain and deliver independence to Cuba. Well, not complete independence, as the American military did occupy the island for years after.

In any case, many Spanish soldiers decided not to go back to Spain but to make Cuba their new home, Ángel Castro among them, which could be seen as an act of rebellion—opting not to return to the country he had been fighting for, and instead making a life among the insurgents who had taken Cuba away from Spain.

Ángel had taken a liking to the island and decided to try to make something of himself in Cuba, which he did. Ultimately, he would amass land and a near-fortune. "No one would ever say that my father was a millionaire . . . although he was very well-to-do and had a solid financial position," Fidel said. "Although in that poor, suffering society we children were treated like the children of rich people . . . a lot of people would come up to us and be nice out of pure self-interest, although we really never realized that."

The political events, still decades before Fidel's birth, were the building blocks of what came to define Fidel. His father's leaving Spain was just a start.

Not having amassed much in his mother country, Angel built up his life in the next decade in Cuba. Within 10 years he was a landowner, and in 1911, he married for the first time. When the marriage failed by the mid 1920s, he left his first wife and five children, and took off with the family cook. This woman, Lina Ruz Gonzalez, originally from the Canary Islands, would give Ángel an additional seven children—Fidel the third-born.

While Ángel and Lina started their life and family together in the '20s, they would not legally marry until 1943—again, not exactly fitting with the mindset of the times. It seems Ángel never planned to marry Lina, but the very Catholic Lina pushed for it. Once Angel's first marriage was officially and finally over, almost 20 years after he left his first wife, he no longer had a choice.

So, it would seem that Fidel's urge to rebel had come from both his father and his mother, who, even as a Catholic, had managed to have an illicit union and family for 20 years, when one could well imagine this was not how she had been raised. But while all sources indicate Fidel had a close relationship with his mother, his relationship with his father was "at arm's length." Fidel said, "Home represented authority and that got my dander up, and the rebel spirit in me began to emerge."

It has been reported that Fidel was somewhat rambunctious as a youth, which was what, in part, prompted his parents to send him off to boarding school. Why had Fidel given his parents such a hard time?

"I had several reasons for being [a rebel]," he said. "Faced with certain Spanish authoritarianism, and even more so the particular Spaniard [his father] giving the orders . . . it was authority, respect in general . . . I didn't like authority, because at that time there was also a lot of corporeal punishment, a slap on the head or a belt taken to you—we always ran the risk, even though we gradually learned to defend ourselves against it."

So the early "injustice" Fidel experienced in his home was not at all about poverty, but about authority, another entity he would grow to rise against. The more educated he became, the more his rebellious streak began to turn into more of a defining trait.

The push for education had come mostly from his mother. Lina came from nothing in every way, and she wanted her children to have everything she did not have. Education, even for Fidel's sisters, was a vital part of that plan. Fidel said, "My mother was practically illiterate, and, like my father, she learned to read and write practically on her own. With a great deal of effort and determination, too. I never heard her say that she'd gone to school. She was self-taught. And extraordinarily hard-working woman, and there was nothing that escaped her attention . . ."

Fidel reported that his relationship with his mother was close and that she was outwardly more loving and affectionate with the children, but "she didn't spoil us, though. She was a stickler for order, savings, cleanliness . . . Nobody knew how she got the time and energy to do everything she did. She never sat down. I never saw her rest one second of the whole day."

When the Spanish Civil War broke out in 1936, Fidel was just shy of 10 years old. At the time, he was home in Birán for a summer break and he learned about the war by reading the newspaper to the cook, Manuel Garcia. Castro recalled: "It had been a pro-Spanish newspaper since the War of Independence and it was the most right-wing of any newspaper that ever existed in the country down to the triumph of the Revolution . . . I would read it to Garcia for hours on end."

So by age 10, Fidel was already starting to understand the difference between the establishment and the rebellion; between keeping the status quo and forging for progress; and the position of the Nationalists, supported by the likes of Hitler and Mussolini, and the driving force behind the Spanish Republic. And he was already beginning to form his opinions—seeds of ideas began to take root and grow. He acquired the facts by reading the papers to Garcia, but then processed the information on his own.

By this time, thanks to the corporeal punishment at home and at school, Fidel had for years already begun to think against the establishment. "I remember well those schoolhouse tortures, although they didn't happen every day, or even all that often. They were really more just ways of scaring us . . . By that time I was already very rebellious . . . I found myself needing to solve problems at a very early age, and that helped me acquire a sense of injustice . . ."

That sense of injustice became the filter through which he understood the events of the war, and informed which side he chose.

Even as a child, he began to act in a kind of violent manner against those whom he felt oppressed him. He recalled a time that one of his teachers got married and honeymooned in Niagara Falls, and this was all she talked about for what seemed like weeks to a roomful of children who may or may not have had enough to eat that day, let alone any sense of what a "luxury vacation" was. Fidel recalled "storming" the teacher's home. "Our first act of vengeance, you might say revenge, and it was with a slingshot . . . We'd made slingshots out of a forked branch of a guava tree and some strips of rubber. There was a bakery nearby, and we took all the firewood for the oven and made ourselves a parapet, a fort, and we organized a bombardment that lasted like half an hour . . . Oh, we were vengeful little devils."

When Fidel was around 11 years old, there was the incident involving his vice principal, which prompted his parents to pull him and his siblings out of school at Christmas. Fidel was incensed that his parents believed the school authorities over him, and he demanded to go back. "I won't accept you not letting me study," he told them. Still, it looked like they were not going to send them back. Fidel needed to give them incentive. "I said that if they didn't send me back to school I was going to burn the house down," he says. "I must have said it very seriously because I was determined to put up a fight against that injustice that was being done against me at school and at home."

Suffice to say, Castro, along with his siblings, returned to school.

In the years to come, those seeds of rebellion took root and sprouted into the man he would become. "I faced certain problems even as a young child, and little by little I developed—that may, indeed, explain my role as a rebel. You hear people talk about 'rebels without a cause', but it seems to me, as I think back over it, I was a rebel with many causes, and I'm grateful to life that I've been able, throughout all these years, to continue to be one."

CHAPTER THREE

THE STUDENT REBEL

"I was a dreadful, terrible example as a student, because I never went to classes. In high school . . . I never attended a lesson . . . At the university, I never went to class, either. What I'd do was talk to the other students in the park, in the Patio de los Laureles. I'd just talk out there—there were small benches—with the guys, and especially with the girls, because they paid a little more attention to me, they were better educated. There were always several students around listening while I explained my theories."

It's funny that for as much as Fidel craved education, he was not an ideal student in any sense of the word. For him, school was about learning, but it was more about "connecting."

Even in high school, Fidel Castro was starting to "find his wings." Though in his case, it was the Left Wing he was finding—and finding it more and more attractive the more he learned and the older he got. Despite not being a stellar student, Castro was still a voracious learner, and read countless books on his own, among them *The Communist Manifesto,* the book that justified his ideas.

He did have to go to class sometimes, however, so he didn't fail out of school, so when he needed to attend, he said, "I just let my imagination fly." As for his studies, he learned everything he needed to know to pass his classes by cramming the nights before exams.

More significant to Fidel's destiny than what he would learn in the classroom was how he was growing politically. His discussions with other students in the courtyard while he avoided classes was only part of this. "What I had was a rebellious spirit, hungry for ideas and knowledge, filled with curiosity and energy," he said. "I sensed from a very young age that there were a great many things to do [in my life]."

If he was testing his wings in high school, the guiding principles of his life would really begin to take shape in college. Castro started university in September 1945, with a deep sense of guilt that many who had grown up around him were never able to complete their education beyond sixth grade, even the best students. It was money that decided who would have the opportunity to continue their education, and thus, the opportunity to succeed. Even though Fidel came from money, and was one of the students who would be given the opportunity to succeed, he lamented, "Was I better than any of those hundreds of poor kids in Birán , almost none of whom ever reached the sixth grade and none of whom graduated high school, none of whom entered university?"

This sense of guilt was part of it. Another part of the equation, however, was his father's firm Right Wing footing—and

Fidel's need to rebel against the authoritarianism of his father at all costs.

But his privilege made him an anomaly among his left-wing oriented peers. "The leftists saw me as a queer duck. They'd say, 'Son of a landowner and a graduate of the Colegio de Belen, this guy must be the most reactionary person in the world.'"

Reactionary or not, politics became the defining force in Fidel's life and his dedication to it surpassed anything else he might be engaged in, including sports. Castro said, "I dedicated my life entirely to politics." He ran for student representative and won the election in a landslide—181 to 33

Once ensconced in that world, he only wished to go further and further. Next was a run for the FEU, the University Student Federation. It was around this time that he started to imagine his place in the world of politics beyond the cocoon of college, and while at university, he opposed the government's candidate for Federation president. The situation became dangerous, and could have been deadly.

Castro said, "I started to strongly oppose the government's candidate. That translated into countless dangers for me, because it ran counter to the interests of the mafia that . . . dominated the university." The situation became so bad, he was practically shut out of school. "I couldn't enter any university facilities," he recalls. "I was up against all powers and all the impunities. They were armed and they had no scruples about killing; they had the support of all the police agencies and Grau's corrupt administration. The only thing that had contained them [so far] had been a moral force, the growing mass of students who supported me. No one had faced them openly in their feudal empire at the university, and they weren't going to tolerate any more defiance, any more challenges to their authority. They also had the university police on their side. I ran the real risk of being killed in what would be alleged to be inter-group rivalry. I cried, but I decided to go back—to go back to fight even though I was aware that it might mean my death."

Around this time, Castro's eyes were definitely also widening beyond the situation in Cuba, and he began to start to consider world politics—Cuba's place in the world, including its strengths and what might be holding it back.

In the late 1940s, he joined the Cayo Confites Expedition. Here, he and like-minded students underwent military training to take down Dominican Republic dictator Rafael Trujillo. Trujillo, or as he was known, El Jefe, had been the leader of the Dominican Republic since 1930, and his nearly 30-year reign was considered one of the bloodiest in the history of the Dominican Republic. While the country prospered under his perceived tyranny, there were no civil liberties for anyone, and the wealth seemed only to go to Trujillo and a small circle of his family, friends, and other supporters.

By this time, Fidel had been appointed chairman of the FEU's Committee for Dominican Democracy, and, Castro said, "I'd taken those responsibilities very seriously . . . I was convinced, on the basis of experience in Cuba, the wars of independence, and other analyses, that you could fight against a conventional modern army by using the methods of irregular warfare. My idea was a guerrilla struggle in the mountains of the Dominican Republic, instead of launching a badly trained, inexperienced force again Trujillo's regular army."

While the attack on Trujillo was not exactly a success, the idea of fighting against a "conventional modern army" with "irregular warfare" became the foundation of so many other rebellions that Castro would soon lead.

In April of 1948, when Colombian presidential candidate Jorge Eliécer Gaitán was shot to death outside of his office in Bogotá, the poor of the city, whose interests the liberal candidate had at heart, began rioting, looting, and murdering in what would come to be known as "El Bogotazo." Three thousand lives were lost in the chaos, and Bogotá was destroyed.

El Bogotazo affected Fidel deeply, especially as he had been a part of it. It showed him that when people were too far oppressed, when their only hope of freedom from that depression was murdered in the street, bad things would happen. "[El Bogotazo] was an experience of great political importance," Castro recalled. "Gaitán represented hope and development for Colombia. His death detonated an explosion—the uprising of the people, a people seeking justice . . . I joined the people. I grabbed a rifle in a police station that collapsed when it was rushed by a crowd. I witnessed the spectacle of a totally spontaneous popular revolution . . . [The experience of El Bogotazo] led me to identify myself even more with the cause of the people."

If the attack on Trujillo and the chaos of El Bogotazo sparked Fidel's desire to unseat injustice in a kind of physical way, it was *The Communist Manifesto* that sparked his intellect. "It made an enormous impact on me," he explained. "I started to see and understand certain things, because I'd been born on a *latifundio*, which was, in addition, surrounded by other huge *latifundios*, and I knew what life was like for those people. I had the experience, at first hand, of what imperialism was domination, one government subservient to another government that was corrupt and repressive."

While in college, Fidel married Mirta Diaz-Balart, who hailed from a wealthy Havana family. One year later, Fidel's son, Fidel ("Fidelito") was born.

When Fidel graduated in 1950, armed now with knowledge and experience and an irrepressible passion to liberate the oppressed, he set up a law practice in Havana and began in earnest his political career.

CHAPTER FOUR

CASTRO AND CHIBAS

"The telegraph operator's son was one of the first people to betray us when the struggle against Batista started. He was a compañero. He lived here in Havana . . . he was a friend, a supporter—he sympathized with us, [he was] in the Party. I trusted him. That's the mistake. You shouldn't trust someone just because he's a friend."

Even in those early years, the backbone of his Fidel's political doctrine—independence, political and economic freedom, and true emancipation—were leading his charge. While at university, Fidel joined the Cuban Orthodox Revolutionary Party, a political party that was headed by Eduardo René Chibás Ribas. Ribas had started the party, known in Cuba as the Ortodoxos party, to use the constitution to bring about revolutionary change—to expose government corruption and give the power to the people.

While Fidel had considered Chibás a mentor, and someone he wanted to follow, there was a fatal flaw in Chibás's makeup: He was anti-Communism. Still, there were tenets on which

Fidel and Chibás were in total alignment, and soon after joining the party, Fidel found himself leader of their Radical Action Group, a smaller offshoot of the Ortodoxos party that included Castro and about 50 other dedicated individuals.

Born in 1907 in Santiago de Cuba, Chibás was a politician with a popular and prominent weekly radio show he used as a forum to blast corruption and gang culture in Cuba. He believed government corruption was the root of all evil. Castro said of Chibás, "[He] wanted to sweep the thieves out of government. And once in a while, he would denounce an 'octopus'—the electricity company, the phone company—when there was some rate increase. He was an advanced thinker in civic terms, but revolutionary social change was not his main objective."

This was another area where the two clashed, but not significantly. All in all, it was in Fidel's best interests to keep aligned with Chibás, who, aside from being against communism, was about all the other things Fidel was about. Though even at this point, Fidel was starting to believe that "revolutionary social change" was the only way that change came about; not by talking on the radio.

However, Chibás wasn't against all action. He did run for president in 1948, placing third, and became a strong critic of the elected president, Carlos Prío Socarrás, for almost his entire tenure in office.

And Chibás's most dramatic radio statement, most dramatic life statement, was all action; there were no words at all.

In August of 1951, Chibás had found himself embroiled in a scandal and there seemed no way to escape. As Castro recalled, "Chibás had denounced the minister of education [Aureliano Sanchez Arango], who was a person with some degree of political acumen, political experience, and who in his time had fought against [Gerardo] Machado and [Fulgencio] Batista, as both a student and professor—he'd been on the Left . . . [He had been] accused by Chibás of owning farms in Guatemala. So, this man defied Chibás, quite spectacularly, to prove it. And Chibás couldn't. Apparently, some source he'd trusted had given him that information without providing the necessary proof."

It was a terrible strain on Chibás and the situation really, in his eyes, ruined his political career and his life, extinguishing any hope he had that he could be the voice to lead the righteous to taking over the Right. Castro said of the scandal that "[Chibás] came under terrible pressure; he was accused of lying and slander. So he fell into a terrible depression and shot himself in the stomach."

It was the how of Chibás shooting himself that really made a statement though. On Aug. 5, 1951, Chibás was supposed to deliver this "proof" he had of Arango's wrongdoings on the air. It was what he had promised his listeners, and he was not going to be able to do it. So he decided to try to make a statement with a gunshot instead.

As what was to be a dramatic apology to his listeners for taking what could only now be considered hearsay and blowing it out of proportion, Chibás was set to take his own life—and do it while he was on the air. Unfortunately for him, but perhaps luckily for his listenership at large, Chibás inadvertently pulled the trigger during the commercial break, and while it looked for a while like he might survive, he died in the hospital 11 days later.

Castro said, "Chibás's dramatic death gave great impetus to the party he'd founded, but the fact that there were no more denunciations made it easier for Batista, whom Chibás had constantly denounced, to carry out his coup. Chibás was a popular figure who'd have been able to offer some resistance to the usurper's coup."

Following Eduardo Chibás's suicide, Castro was instrumental in holding together the Cuban Orthodox party, and used what could have dissolved into chaos and despair as a stepping stone to become the Ortodoxos candidate in the 1952 election.

But despite having been aligned with Chibás inhiss early political career, something did not sit right for Fidel about Chibás and his loyalty to the cause. And while it would have been impossible to blame Chibás for the later unsuccessful taking down of President Batista via the Moncada attacks, there was something about his association with the group that never seemed to quite sit right with Fidel.

Regarding the earlier traitorous statement Fidel seemingly made about the man whom he had considered a friend, "We were using a mimeograph machine to print up a clandestine newspaper, a flier, a manifesto, trying to create a clandestine revolutionary publication and also a radio station, using short wave radio . . . This son of Valero's informed Batista's police of—I believe I am correct—the location of the mimeograph machine we were using to print up our little newspaper, *El Acusador (The Accuser)*. That's where I published our first manifest, which I wrote a year after Chibás's death, on 16 August 1952, four months after Batista's military coup."

Whatever the cause, Fidel knew even then that the risks of their endeavor might well outweigh the reward, but the risks had to be taken, and with great force and fury, if change was ever going to come.

CHAPTER FIVE

CASTRO VS. BATISTA

"On my own I came to the conclusion that the capitalist economy was absurd. What I'd already become, before I came into contact with Marxist or Lenin material, was a utopian Communist. A utopian Communist is someone whose ideas don't have any basis in science or history, but who sees that things are very bad, who sees poverty, injustice, inequality, and insuperable contradiction between society and true development . . . When people talk about the 'crisis of overproduction' and the 'crisis of unemployment' and other problems, I gradually came to the conclusion that the system didn't work."

Not only did Castro believe the capitalist system didn't work, he believed it needed to be abolished, the years and his increasing level of education only supporting what he fundamentally knew inside to be true. *Some* of the people should not be hoarding *all* the wealth and resources for themselves, especially when there was no real fairness in how those resources came to be hoarded, except through the fact that the people who controlled the wealth and the power held on to the wealth and the power. All that was going to change in Castro's Cuba, though it wouldn't happen with one sweeping overnight change as Castro would have liked. It would take years, cost lives, and even cost Castro years of his life in prison. But we'll get to all that in a bit.

Following the death of Chibás, Fidel became the Ortodoxos party candidate for president. Also running in the 1952 election was former president Fulgencio Batista Zaldívar. Batista had ruled over the island country between 1940 and 1944, elected on the populist platform. He instated the 1940 Constitution of Cuba, which, at the time, was progressive, and ruled the country without much chaos at home. The world was at war, after all, and people were focused globally, more than on their own private national interests. After his rule ended in 1944, Batista moved to the United States, and wasn't heard from again until the early 1950s.

While Batista was enjoying all the creature comforts of capitalism in the United States, remember that these years, 1944-1952, were incredibly formative for Castro. He already had his ideals, the ones that were already a part of him from a young age. As Castro said, "I think that very early on, in school, at home, I started to see and live through things that were unfair, unjust. I'd been born on a large tract of land in the country, and I knew how that was. I have an indelible memory of what capitalism was in the country. The images of so many poor, hard-working, humble people . . . hungry, barefoot . . . especially the men and women who worked for the large American sugar companies . . . they would come to my father and ask for his help."

The knowledge Fidel received outside his high school and

college classrooms was more important, more significant to him, than anything he took in from books and lessons. To continue the seed metaphor, the case had cracked, the roots were deep, and the sprout of what this life would be was just about to peek out. "Little by little I began to acquire notions of justice and dignity, certain central values," he said. "So my character was molded by the hard tests I had to pass, difficulties I had to overcome, conflicts I had to face, decisions I had to make, rebellions . . . I started to question that society on my own . . . With no one to help me, really."

Well, perhaps as a child, growing up in a right-wing, wealthy, capitalism-benefitting sprawling homestead, there was no one there to help him, except maybe the cook for whom he had read newspapers, the cook whose illiteracy had gained Fidel a wealth of knowledge about the workings of the world. And also his authoritarian father, whose corporal punishments had shown Fidel how authority sometimes abused its place, and the teachers Fidel had encountered who had strengthened this idea for Fidel. "Very early on, all those experiences led me to see the abuses, the injustice, or the simple humiliation of another person as inconceivable wrongs. I began to acquire awareness. I never resigned myself to abuses. I acquired a profound sense of justice, ethics, a sense of equality. All that, in addition to a temperament that was unquestionably rebellious, must have exerted a strong influence on my political and revolutionary vocation."

Could it be more well timed that the year that Fidel was ready to begin his political career, to really start moving and shaking with a decision to run for office in the 1952 elections, that Batista decided to come back to Cuba to run for president again? And when he decided he was probably not going to get elected, to take over the country by military coup?

Yet this is precisely what happened. In the midst of Fidel's realizations within himself that he needed to take on tyranny with his bare hands, that he needed to be the force that forced out government corruption, this former president came back and not only reclaimed the government by force, but actually suspended the constitution he had put in place 12 years before and revoked the people's political liberties. He would then aligned himself with wealth in the country, and worked to elevate the richest to more wealth, and worked to further oppress the poor. Could there be a better time for Fidel to begin his mission? His movement to revolution?

Castro said, "That movement began not with the intention of carrying out a revolution all by ourselves, but rather on the basis of another premise: Everyone would fight to return to the situation prior to 10 March, and with that to the constitutional and political situation destroyed by the coup."

In the months following the coup, the economy stagnated, Batista's regime became increasingly corrupt and repressive and poisoned Cuba's commercial interests through exploitative practices involving drug trafficking, prostitution, and just general badness.

The people were upset. Riots and demonstrations broke out in spite of Batista revoking the people's rights to demonstrate. Censorship was rampant, and Batista's anti-communist police tortured and executed nearly 20,000 Cuban citizens. It was a mess.

Castro said, "I believed everyone would come together to wipe out Batista's tyranny. It was clear to me that Batista had to be overthrown by arms and that constitutional government had to be restored. To me it was simple: Join hands to fight the traitorous coup of the 10th of March. Until that day, I, who had pretty well-formed idea of what should be done . . . was using legal means, although they led, on the basis of my ideas, to the idea or the revolutionary seizure of power. The coup destroyed all that. In the new situation . . . I thought, to return to the starting point."

Almost immediately, Fidel and his followers began in earnest to set a plan in motion to overthrow the tyrant and return Cuba back to the people. It was no longer time for talking and playing fair; it was time to take all resources available and begin the revolution. Said Castro of himself and his contingent of dedicated followers, "If we hadn't studied Marxism . . . if we hadn't read Marx's books on political theory, and if we hadn't been inspired by Marti, Marx, and Lenin, we couldn't possibly have conceived the idea of a revolution in Cuba, because with a group of men, none of whom has gone through a military academy, you can't wage a war against a well-organized, well-armed, well-trained army and win a victory starting practically from scratch. Those ideas were the essential building blocks of the revolution."

In a year's time, Fidel and his men would believe themselves ready to take down the Batista regime. Though, thanks to what Fidel believes to have been some communication leaks within the ranks, they would be more surprised by their "surprise" attack on the Moncada Barracks than their enemies.

CHAPTER SIX

PLANNING THE MONCADA BARRACKS ATTACKS

"I must pause to consider the facts for a moment. The government itself said the attack showed such precision and perfection that it must have been planned by military strategists. Nothing could have been farther from the truth! The plan was drawn up by a group of young men, none of whom had any military experience at all. I will reveal their names, omitting two who are neither dead nor in prison: Abel Santamaría, José Luis Tasende, Renato Guitart Rosell, Pedro Miret, Jesús Montané, and myself. Half of them are dead, and in tribute to their memory I can say that although they were not military experts they had enough patriotism to have given, had we not been at such a great disadvantage, a good beating to that entire lot of generals together, those generals of the 10th of March who are neither soldiers nor patriots. Much more difficult than the planning of the attack was

our organizing, training, mobilizing and arming men under this repressive regime with its millions of dollars spent on espionage, bribery and information services. Nevertheless, all this was carried out by those men and many others like them with incredible seriousness, discretion and discipline. Still more praiseworthy is the fact that they gave this task everything they had; ultimately, their very lives."

—From his speech HISTORY WILL ABSOLVE ME, a reconstruction of Fidel Castro's statements in court after the failed Moncada Barracks attack.

While Fidel Castro had been involved in political movements since his early college years, he took his first true steps onto the world stage on July 26, 1953, with his attack on the Moncada military barracks in Santiago, Cuba. The attack failed and many of Castro's soldiers were killed, but the bold ambush put Castro in a position to broadcast his views and revolutionary ideas from his jail cell.

Castro made his move soon after Fulgencia Batista's military coup on March 10, 1953. The political climate was tense, and few groups spoke out openly against Batista's regime; however, Castro released a manifesto soon after speaking out against the unjust transfer of power. Castro later described the situation. "When did we decide to attack Moncada? When we became convinced that nobody was going to do anything, that there was not going to be any fight against Batista, and that many of the existing groups—in which there were lots and lots of people who were members of several [groups] at the same time—were not prepared, not organized, to carry out the armed struggle that I was hoping for."

While the attack may have gone poorly for Castro and his men, the planning for the offensive went much more smoothly. Castro was able to recruit, train, and outfit his army right under the nose of Batista's regime without giving them any warning before the day of the attack.

Castro's soldiers were mostly young members of the Cuban Orthodox Revolutionary Party, which Castro had joined in 1947, and under which he had run for office in 1952, before Batista's coup.

The young recruits required training, but it was to be done covertly, so as not to raise the regime's suspicions. Instead of setting up a training camp somewhere out of the way, Castro explains that the men were trained in Havana, in the open. "Do you know where we trained to learn to shoot rifles? . . . [A]t firing ranges in Havanah. We disguised some of our *compañeros* as good upstanding members of the bourgeoisie—businessmen, whatever, depending on what you looked like, your style, your abilities. We'd register them first, for example, in hunting clubs, and they'd invite us to their clubs to practice clay-pigeon shooting."

The day before the attack, Castro and his men met at a farm near Santiago to organize and to give final orders for the attack. They disguised the farm so no one would suspect it to be the launch point for their attack, even setting up a fake chicken coop and planting extra trees to hide their cars from being seen from the air. At the farm they also handed out uniforms; they were to be dressed in the same uniforms as Batista's men, all with the rank of sergeant. They had bought and sewn enough uniforms for everyone, and only their shoes were their own.

They set off from the farm early the next morning and headed for the Moncada Barracks in Santiago. Fidel lead a group of 160 men and women, mostly members of the Ortodoxos party, while another group went to another army post near Bayamo. Fidel had chosen these targets for his surprise attack so that the group could obtain more weapons before retreating into the mountains, according to Naty Revuelta, an Ortodoxos member who later had a close personal relationship and a daughter with Castro. The timing was chosen to coincide with festivals in the city, which made their movements easier as many visitors and tourists came and went from Santiago. Everything was ready: The plan was to arrive at the barracks early, as they expected the soldiers to be sleeping, perhaps even hungover from the celebrations the night before. Castro explained the plan. "The soldiers were going to be asleep and they'd be pushed out of the barracks dormitories into the rear courtyard . . . The soldiers were going to be in their underwear because they wouldn't have had time to get dressed or pick up their weapons." But the plan was disrupted quickly as a pair of soldiers on patrol spotted Castro's men and alerted the guard post. A number of other setbacks quickly ended the offensive: Alarms rang out, Castro's men got lost and mistook their objectives, and everything fell into disorganization and chaos. Castro realized their plan had failed and ordered a retreat.

In many ways, the attack on the Moncada Barracks was a complete failure for Castro. Many of his men were killed and tortured by their captors, and the popular uprising Castro expected from the people of Santiago never materialized. Still, the attack was eventually considered the "first shot" in the Cuban revolution, and the date became a rallying cry for Castro's supporters, with Castro taking the name "the 26th of July Movement" for his political movement that later unseated Batista. Castro said later, reflecting on the attack, "If I were to organize a plan for taking the Moncada Barracks again, I would do it exactly the same way. I wouldn't change a thing. What failed there was that we lacked sufficient combat experience. Later, we picked it up . . ." It served as an important step in Castro's ascent to power, a learning experience that put him in the public eye.

CHAPTER SEVEN

ABSOLVED BY HISTORY

"Since this trial may, as you said, be the most important trial since we achieved our national sovereignty, what I say here will perhaps be lost in the silence which the dictatorship has tried to impose on me, but posterity will often turn its eyes to what you do here. Remember that today you are judging an accused man, but that you yourselves will be judged not once, but many times, as often as these days are submitted to scrutiny in the future. What I say here will be then repeated many times, not because it comes from my lips, but because the problem of justice is eternal and the people have a deep sense of justice above and beyond the hairsplitting of jurisprudence. The people wield simple but implacable logic, in conflict with all that is absurd and contradictory. Furthermore, if there is in this world a people that utterly abhors favoritism and inequality, it is the Cuban people. To them, justice is symbolized by a maiden with a scale and a sword in her hands. Should she cower before one group and furiously wield that sword against another group, then to the people of Cuba the maiden of justice

*will seem nothing more than a prostitute brandishing a
dagger. My logic is the simple logic of the people. [. . .]
I know that imprisonment will be harder for me than it
has ever been for anyone, filled with cowardly threats
and hideous cruelty. But I do not fear prison, as I do not
fear the fury of the miserable tyrant who took the lives
of 70 of my comrades. Condemn me. It does not matter.
History will absolve me."*

—*HISTORY WILL ABSOLVE ME: Fidel Castro's
speech in court, defending himself and his revolution*

After the failed Moncada Barracks attack, Castro and a few
other survivors fled to the mountains to escape capture. They
were tired, and some were wounded, and they were pursued
by Batista's soldiers, and it wasn't long until they were captured. Some sources give credit to the local Catholic bishop
for speaking out for prisoners' rights and saving Castro's
life, but Castro offers another story in his later recounting
of the events. He describes how he and his comrades slept
in an abandoned shack one night, only to wake to the sound
of hoofbeats and the door being bashed open. The soldiers
were excited, and Castro thought they wanted to shoot
him, but their leader, a lieutenant, told them, "Don't shoot,
don't shoot. Ideas can't be killed." Castro claims this same
lieutenant refused to turn Castro over to his superior, and
instead brought Castro back to Santiago, even after Castro
had revealed who he was.

Once he was in jail awaiting trial, Castro took every opportunity he could to get his message out to the people of Cuba.
In September 1953, Fidel and another 100 defendants were

charged with "leading an attempt aimed at organizing an uprising of armed persons against constitutional powers of the state." Castro acted as his own lawyer, but after five days of trial the court claimed he was too sick to continue, and sent him back to jail. In a later interview, Castro explained what had them so upset. "[W]hen the trial started, on Monday 21 September 1953, I assumed my own defense. And as [the defense] lawyer I started interrogating all those thugs and henchmen, all the witnesses, and that was a sight to see . . . They couldn't take it; they pulled me out of the trial because they couldn't prevent my denunciations. They tried me later by myself, with another man who'd been wounded, in a little room in the hospital." Despite their attempts to keep him quiet, Castro had his day in court. He delivered an impassioned defense, citing abuses by Batista's soldiers and placing his actions firmly in a historical context, and arguing clearly for the righteousness of his actions.

In Castro's famous defense speech, he spoke directly against the charges, arguing that he was not guilty of leading an uprising against the constitutional powers of the state. He said he had taken up arms against the Batista regime, which he argued was not a constitutional government at all, as Batista was not elected, but took his power by force. Castro had plenty of criticism for the Batista regime, even comparing them to the Nazis. "The regime has reached the point of asserting that 'Might makes right' is the supreme law of the land. In other words, that using tanks and soldiers to take over the presidential palace, the national treasury, and the other government offices, and aiming guns at the heart of the people, entitles them to govern the people!"

Castro also addressed the Batista regime's violent abuses following the Moncada Barracks attack, when captured men were tortured and executed. He offered many accounts of the regime's cruelty in his speech, describing how they tore wounded men from the doctors' care and let them die, and how they tried to force one of the women in Castro's group to give them information by bringing her her brother's eye, cut from his head. He explains what happened to many of the men who survived the battle, but were captured by the soldiers:

"In the early morning hours, groups of our men were removed from the barracks and taken in automobiles to Siboney, La Maya, Songo, and elsewhere. Then they were led out—tied, gagged, already disfigured by the torture—and were murdered in isolated spots. They are recorded as having died in combat against the Army. This went on for several days, and few of the captured prisoners survived. Many were compelled to dig their own graves."

Castro also criticized Batista's regime for how it had led the country, saying that his leadership had not made things better for the Cuban people, but had only benefitted Batista's financial interests and those of his closest supporters. Castro didn't hold back his criticism, saying, "Little else could be expected from a man of his mentality—utterly devoid as he is of ideals and of principles, and utterly lacking the faith, confidence, and support of the masses."

In contrast, Castro frames his fight as the fight for the common people. Despite the fact that the Moncada attacks had not sparked a popular uprising, as he had hoped, Castro still claimed to have the will of the people on his side. His defense, aside from providing a solid counter to the regime's charges, served to put Castro's fight into a historical context, and claim the support of his people. When asked if the Moncada attacks could be called the first battle of the Cuban Revolution, Castro said in a later interview, "That wouldn't be completely fair, because the Cuban Revolution began with the first War of Independence in 1868, which started in Oriente province on 10 October of that year." In his speech, Castro deftly connected his movement to the national narrative, framing his offensive as the next step in the long battle for independence, and arguing that his actions were not only just, but necessary. Castro called on strong patriotic themes when he said, "We are Cubans and to be Cuban implies a duty; not to fulfill that duty is a crime, is treason. We are proud of the history of our country; we learned it in school and have grown up hearing of freedom, justice, and human rights. [...]

"We were taught that the 10th of October and the 24th of February are glorious anniversaries of national rejoicing because they mark days on which Cubans rebelled against the yoke of infamous tyranny. We were taught to cherish and defend the beloved flag of the lone star, and to sing every afternoon the verses of our National Anthem: 'To live in chains is to live in disgrace and in opprobrium,' and 'to die for one's homeland is to live forever!' All this we learned and will never forget, even though today in our land there is murder and prison for the men who practice the ideas taught to them since the cradle. We were born in a free country that our parents bequeathed to us, and the Island will first sink into the sea before we consent to be the slaves of anyone."

Despite his impassioned defense, Castro was found guilty and sentenced to 15 years at the Isla de Pinos, where his brother Raul and other surviving allies were already imprisoned.

Officials did not want to give Castro any more opportunity to spread his political message, so the trial was conducted quickly and with little fanfare. Still, soon after he was put in jail, Castro released a copy of his testimony, rewritten from his recollections. The manifesto, called HISTORY WILL ABSOLVE ME, takes its name from the stirring closing line of his speech, in which Castro said, "I know that imprisonment will be harder for me than it has ever been for anyone, filled with cowardly threats and hideous cruelty. But I do not fear prison, as I do not fear the fury of the miserable tyrant who took the lives of 70 of my comrades. Condemn me. It does not matter. History will absolve me." As many as 10,000 copies of the speech were printed and distributed to the people of Cuba, solidly establishing Castro as the primary rival to Batista's rule.

CHAPTER EIGHT

IMPRISONED

"I would honestly love to revolutionize this country from one end to the other! I am sure this would bring happiness to the Cuban people. I would not be stopped by the hatred and ill will of a few thousand people, including some of my relatives, half the people I know, two-thirds of my fellow professionals, and four-fifths of my ex-schoolmates."

The failed attempt to attack the Moncada Barracks. The long trial that ended in sentencing for long prison terms for himself, his brother, Raul, and more than 20 other co-conspirators. The bleak reality of prison. None of this took Fidel Castro away from his plan to overthrow Batista. Said Castro during his trial, "The only remedy to force without authority is to oppose it with force" and that "a government acclaimed by the mass of combatants would receive and be vested with the necessary power to establish effectively the will of the people and true justice." The only way that Castro and his *compañeros* were going to be able to take Cuba out of Batista's hands was through the same means Batista had taken power: violence.

Being in prison would not deter Fidel; in fact, doing time was almost a retreat for planning and scheming. It was a perfect venue for Fidel to collect his thoughts without many distractions. To organize his ideas. To begin laying the groundwork to set the next attack in motion—and this time, make it a successful attack. "What a fantastic school this prison is!" the barely 30-year-old wrote optimistically in a letter from his cell. "Here I have forged my vision of the world and found the meaning of my life."

Even as he began to serve his 15-year sentence, he knew two things: that he would not be in prison forever, and that when he got out, he would already have the means in place to take Batista down. As he wrote to his sister (from his father's first family) from his cell, "Don't worry about me; you know I have a heart of steel and that I will be stalwart till the last day of my life. Nothing has been lost!" That optimism and his determination to set right the original plan of his failed Moncada mission kept him focused.

Fidel made the most of his time, planning and getting everything in order for what would come to be called the "26th of July Movement," which had been the date of the failed Moncada attack.

Even incarcerated, Fidel remained in charge, corresponding with supporters on the outside and continuing to build a base of revolutionaries to join his army. Though there were times when the situation frustrated him:

"To be a prisoner is to be condemned to silence, to hear and read everything spoken and not be able to speak out, to endure the attacks of cowards who take advantage of the circumstances to fight those who cannot defend themselves and to make accusations that would merit our immediate response, were it not physically impossible."

On the inside, Fidel led. He engaged regularly with inmates, educating them and motivating them. He even created a school for the prisoners, calling it the Abel Santamaría Ideological Academy, named for his *compañero* and fellow revolutionary who had, along with his sister, Haydee Santamaría, fought alongside Fidel at Moncada. Abel had also been captured, but was murdered in prison in 1953. In Fidel's "school," he taught subjects like history, philosophy, and introduced student-inmates to the *Communist Manifesto*, among other works he valued.

For his own education, Fidel continued to learn the way he always had in school—on his own, through books. When he wasn't teaching, and when he wasn't planning the next revolution, he read works by great thinkers, from Shakespeare to Freud, and began analyzing these works to find communist threads in them. One of his favorite concepts for study was FDR's New Deal, the structure of which he hoped to bring to Cuba after a successful revolution.

When Batista himself made a visit to the prison in February of 1954, Fidel organized inmates to protest by singing anti-Batista songs. For that, he was placed in solitary confinement for several months. But even isolated, he made impact. As he wrote of this portion of his sentence:

"Here I spend my days reading and exercising self-control. I definitely feel better when I do not read the newspapers; the politicking and the conformity I see everywhere produces in me fits of rage. If anyone's patience has been put to the test it's mine; there are times when I spend whole hours fighting the desire to explode or declare myself on hunger strike and not eat a thing until I am taken out of this cell or killed, which is not unlikely. I am convinced that they want to provoke me at all costs, but I don't pay attention to their intentions. Otherwise, why after four months do they persist in keeping me isolated? Nonetheless, I do not know how long I will have the energy to contain myself."

While Fidel and his comrades served their sentences, another presidential selection was set to occur on the outside, at the end of 1954. The trouble, of course, was that no one dared run against Batista, so he won. He was inaugurated in February 1955. This wasn't completely bad for Castro and his incarcerated compatriots, however.

Batista was supposed to restore the Constitution of 1940, but he was slow to act. Because of the widespread anger at what many considered a bogus election, supporters were able to wrangle amnesty for Fidel and the other jailed participants from the Moncada incident, convincing Batista that Fidel and his friends were no political threat, and that the gesture would gain Batista more popular favor.

Also at this time, Cuba had made an arrangement to export sugar to the Soviet Union, and had the blessing of the U.S. president at the time, Dwight D. Eisenhower, delivered in person by Vice President Richard Nixon. All of this, in combination with growing prosperity in Cuba, convinced Batista that amnesty was the way to go.

On May 15, 1955, Fidel, Raul, and the rest of the Moncada members were released from prison. Fidel returned to Havana, where he gave interviews about Moncada, about his time in prison, and about his release. In Havana, he continued the work he had begun while locked away, to take down Batista once and for all. It wasn't easy, however; he was under pretty much constant surveillance from the government who may have released him but did not trust him.

Still, Fidel forged ahead. He established a National Directorate and lost some supporters who felt that Fidel seemed more "dictator" than leader. However, most stayed with him, and the planning for the July 26th Movement was in full effect. But because of the ever-watchful government eyes, they were not going to get very far with their planning in Cuba. It was time to find another location to stage the revolution.

CHAPTER NINE

PERSONAL UPHEAVAL

"Mirta is too level-headed to have ever allowed herself to be seduced by her family, agreeing to appear on the government employee roster, no matter how hard her economic situation. I am sure she has been miserably slandered. The nature of this problem is so sad and difficult that I can barely contemplate it. I am ready to clear this up and will do anything to take action against this cowardly insult."

Having a spouse in prison would be a tough cross to bear for anyone in that position, but when your husband has been jailed with a sentence of 15 years, and you have nothing to count on except the family from whom your jailed husband has become estranged, it has to be an enormous strain. So being put on the government payroll by your brother, even a government as corrupt as the one Fidel was raging against, could be understandable. Unless, of course, you're married to Fidel Castro, who considered this, as stated above, to be a "cowardly insult."

Exactly when Fidel became estranged from his family is

not entirely clear, though it may have had to do with his father-in-law, wealthy Havana general Lincoln, becoming Batista's deputy interior minister (and her brother, also named Lincoln, becoming one of Batista's officers). But at the beginning of the relationship, when Fidel and Mirta Diaz-Balart, a philosophy student, were in college, her family seemed in full support of the union. They married on October 11, 1948, and a year later, On September 1, 1949, welcomed a son, Fidel Ángel "Fidelito" Castro Díaz-Balart. It's interesting that Fidel named his son after himself and his father, as of his own given name he has said, "I had no name of my own. I was called Fidel because of somebody [Fidel Pino Santos] who was going to be my godfather." And who, in fact, did not become Fidel's godfather after all.

In any case, there were no issues with Fidel and his bride's new family in the beginning. In fact, his in-laws even paid for the new couple's honeymoon in Miami, Florida, which was, incidentally, the first time Fidel ever visited the United States. However, all was not right with that trip. As some stories report, Fidel ran into some financial issues on the honeymoon and had to pawn some of his belongings until his own family could get money to them.

There didn't seem to have been any real issues between the Castros, though as Batista took over control of the country, with Mirta straddling the line between her family's embracing of the self-mandated president and ruler of Cuba, and her husband's deepest desire to dethrone him, so to speak, there had to have been more than the usual strain between spouse and in-laws.

But it wasn't until Castro's capture and incarceration that

things really began to fray. Mirta took a job at the Ministry of the Interior at the behest of her brother, and did not mention it to her husband. It was a worse betrayal to him than had she been carrying on an affair. Castro did not learn of the employment from his wife or his in-laws; he found out on the radio, and when he did, he could not at first believe what he was hearing. As he wrote in a letter to Luis Conte about the radio broadcast, "I am ready to challenge my brother-in-law to a duel at any time. It is the reputation of my wife and my honor as a revolutionary that is at stake. Do not hesitate: Strike back and have no mercy. I would rather be killed a thousand times over than helplessly suffer such an insult."

The larger insult, of course, would be that the accusation was true. That Mirta had indeed, and without telling her revolutionary husband, taken a job supporting the government that Fidel was now suffering a prison sentence for having attempted to rise up against. He wrote to Luis, "I do not want to become a murderer when I leave prison," and that was when he thought all was against Mirta and him. When he realized that she, too, by this act of her employment, was against him, there was no marriage left, for either party involved.

Both partners filed for divorce, but that wasn't when it got ugly. According to Cuban law at the time, in the event of divorce, custody went to the father. The father was not in a position at the time to take physical custody of Fidelito, so their son stayed with his mother, who had left the country with the boy. Nothing could have ever angered him more than this, his estranged wife's second betrayal. Said Fidel, "I will be free one day and they will have to return my son and my honor, even if the earth shall be destroyed." There was no way he would let her get away with taking his son from him. "I presume they know that to rob me of that boy, they will have to kill me," he wrote in a letter. "And not even then."

A bitter custody battle ensued. There was no way Mirta was handing over her son; there was no way Fidel was going to let her have him. From prison, he wrote, "About the boy, I remain unchanged in my point of view at the first opportunity—immediately after the filing—will press the court to force his return to Cuba to attend school, consistent with my thinking. Such a deep abyss separates me from these people [the Diaz-Balants] that I resist the thought of my son sleeping for one night under the same roof that shelters my most despicable enemies and receiving on his innocent cheeks the kisses of those miserable Judases."

Fidel fought furiously, relying on the only ammunition he had in his arsenal: his words, delivered by his faithful followers, including his older sister from his father's first marriage. He wrote, "I am enough of a gentleman to avoid bitter contest if my kidnapped son is returned to me. I have decided to carry on this bitter legal action wherever it leads if they persist in the foolish fantasy that I would allow them to educate the boy to live as a parasite, without a homeland, without honor, and without principles."

Mirta was finally forced to give up the fight. In 1955, after the divorce was final, she married Emilio Núñez Blanco, and left Cuba and her son behind to live with her new husband in Madrid, Spain. She did eventually return to Cuba while her son was young, before ultimately moving to the U.S.

Fidel had had a reputation of being something of a womanizer, which had affected his marriage when a letter to his mistress ended up with his wife. So the family situation was the kindling for the divorce, but learning there was another woman, and that there could have been several more, is a reason many biographers have attributed to Mirta taking Fidelito out of Cuba.

In any case, once divorced, and then released from prison, however, he was free to do what he wanted. He ended up fathering several illegitimate children, all born to different mothers, the year after his release; all the women were fierce supporters of Castro and his ideals.

CHAPTER TEN

TRAINING AN ARMY IN MEXICO

"We had neither money nor weapons. We had to find a way to overthrow the tyranny and make a revolution in Cuba. And success crowned our venture. I'm not going to tell you that it worked purely on its own merits—luck played an important part."

Once released from prison in 1955, Fidel and Raul returned to Havana; however, it was very clear very early on that there was no way they were going to be able to stage a proper revolution under Batista's ever-watchful eye. They needed another plan. Even while still in prison they decided they would ultimately go to Mexico, as it was a country that had long been friendly to leftist exiles, as well as being a place other Cubans had gone before to stage prior uprisings.

Raul headed to Mexico first, leaving Fidel to get organized in Havana. One of the last things he did was to write a letter to the newspapers, telling them that he was "leaving Cuba because all doors of peaceful struggle have been closed to me.

Six weeks after being released from prison, I am convinced more than ever of the dictatorship's intention, masked in many ways, to remain in power for 20 years, ruling as now by the use of terror and crime and ignoring the patience of the Cuban people, which has its limits. As a follower of Martí, I believe the hour has come to take our rights and not beg for them, to fight instead of pleading for them."

In Mexico, Raul became acquainted with Che Guevera, a young Argentine doctor. Fidel finally arrived in Mexico, and on being introduced to Che, knew the South American would play a large part in what they were trying to accomplish.

The objective in Mexico was to organize, arm, and then ambush. Rigorous training defined days spent in the Sierra Maestra. Castro said, "In Mexico . . . we trained many *compañeros*. I had to do the organizational work and find and acquire weapons, and I was training the men on the firing ranges." He also made trips to the states to secure funds from supporters there, and to acquire more weapons.

Strategies were formed, relying on Castro's vast knowledge, having studied intensely other wars in Cuba. Castro recalled, "[The wars] in Cuba helped us in formulating a different strategy, because both Maceo and Maximo Gomez had cavalry, a very mobile army, and they had virtual freedom of movement . . . Our main combats, however, in the circumstances of our war, were planned, with cover, trenches prepared, all sorts of other essential measures taken."

There was no man among them who had been formerly trained in the military, so it all came down to studying and understanding what had worked in histories of past battles, and lots and lots of practice. "There in Mexico we practiced our marksmanship at a range near Mexico City. It belonged to an old confederate of Pancho Villa's, and he'd leaded it to us. When we disembarked, we had 55 rifles with telescopic sights. Our practice with those rifles consisted of shooting sheep that were turned loose 200 yards out in the firing range—without support for the rifle, free-handed . . . Our men were very good shots. They'd send a man out 200 yards, and put a bottle down on the ground beside him . . . we'd fire hundreds of rounds . . . Those practices gave us complete confidence in what we could do with one of those weapons."

Another effect of the time spent in Mexico preparing to overthrow Batista was that the men began to grow beards, which became, as Castro explained, "a kind of badge of identity." This was only an interesting side-effect, though; the men weren't growing beards for any kind of "branding" reason. "We didn't have any razor blades, or straight razors." Not to mention that it was simply easier to grow a beard than to have to deal with shaving every day. Castro said, "A beard has a practical advantage: you don't have to shave every day. If you multiply the 15 minutes you spend shaving every day by the number of days in a year, you'll see that you devoted almost 5,500 minutes to shaving. An eight-hour day of work consists of 480 minutes, so if you don't shave, you gain about ten days that you can devote to work, to reading, to sport, or whatever you like . . . The only disadvantage is that grey hair show first in your beard."

Castro and his *compañeros* were not left completely alone in while in Mexico. Batista was keeping tabs on them, and was especially interest in a trip Fidel made to the U.S. to secure funding. He ending up collecting about $100,000. Upon his return, some of Batista's agents failed to assassinate him. The agents additionally bribed Mexican authorities to seize the rebels and their camp, but they were soon released.

"Batista had influence among the Secret Police; he'd bought them off, so they supported him, and he had plans to kidnap us in Mexico. We were forced to take counter-measures, so one afternoon, just at nightfall, when we were moving from one house to another, we were exposed, you see, [and] several Federales . . . saw us moving and decided to arrest us. They were pretty sharp, I must say."

What ensued was an arrest during which Castro was captured and, along with others, was brought in for questioning. In speaking with the Federales, Castro gleaned that one of his own people had let a paper slip, which sparked suspicion when it landed in the hands of the police, who followed procedure to follow the trail. "We were captured [in Mexico]. I was taken prisoner almost by chance. A little piece of paper here and another one there that the Mexican police discovered in the pockets of some [of our men] whom they'd arrested . . . They initially thought we were smugglers or something, because we made ourselves look suspicious because of certain measures we took against being kidnapped and killed by Batista's agents [in Mexico]. Our movements look strange to them [the Federales] . . . Thank goodness the police hadn't thought of investigating that telephone number more closely, because that would have been the end. But they still confiscated quite a few weapons by following other clues. You could see, though, that as they got to know us, they began to have more respect for us."

Another interesting development while Castro and his

guerrillas trained in the Sierra Maestra was a general strike against Batista by a militant anti-Batista group formed by the student movement; most notable was the Revolutionary Directorate (DR), founded by the Federation of University Students (FEU). The president, Jose Antonio Echevarria, headed to Mexico to seek Castro's support, but Castro did not come out in favor of the strike. He was too focused on his group's efforts to support the strike, which ultimately failed. The fact of the matter was that sometimes these things happened. "You can make mistakes, commit errors, or do things as perfectly as possible, and there are still things you can't foresee," Castro said.

Castro and crew set sail from Veracruz on November 25, 1956, armed with rifles, machine guns, pistols, and hand-held anti-tank guns. And a strategy was ready to put in motion, a strategy that was years in the making. Recalls Castro: "Even before I went to prison, I had the plan for the war in the Sierra Maestra, the whole plan. We developed a warfare of movement . . . attack and fall back. Surprise. Attack, and attack again. And a great deal of psychological warfare . . . But for us, guerrilla warfare was the detonator of another process whose objective was the revolutionary takeover of power. And with a culminating point: a revolutionary general strike and a general uprising of the populace."

They were on their way.

CHAPTER ELEVEN

CASTRO AND CHE

"[Che] distinguished himself in so many ways, through so many fine qualities . . . As a man, as an extraordinary human being. He was also a person of great culture, a person of great intelligence. And with military qualities as well. Che was a doctor who became a soldier without ceasing for a single minute to be a doctor."

Fidel Castro and Ernesto "Che" Guevara made for an extraordinary team because their personalities clicked. They were contrasting and also complementary. It has been said that Che was Fidel's "brain," but in so many ways, he was the "heart." To best understand the relationship between Fidel and Che, it's important to have some background on Che.

Born in Rosario, Argentina, on June 14, 1928, making him just under two years younger than Fidel, Ernesto Guevara was like Castro in that he came from a large, wealthy family. The oldest of five children, Ernesto was of Basque and Irish descent. His leftist ideals were learned from his parents, who did not lean as far left as he did, but who believed in education and doing right by humanity. From a very early age, he understood the plight of the poor and was compelled to do something. He was also an athlete, despite his sometimes crippling asthma, and an intellectual, and, like Fidel, he read constantly. It is said his parents' home contained more than 3,000 books. He was passionate about poetry, and also a chess champion.

As a student, he had traveled through South America on a motorcycle with a friend, and the experience set the course for the rest of his life. The poverty he witnessed in his travels sparked a desire in him to devote himself to helping those who could not help themselves. And his passion for helping others was contagious. Castro said of Che, "He had a gift for people. He was one of those people that everyone immediately cares about—it was his naturalness, his simplicity, his sense of comradeship and all his virtues."

Once he finished medical school, he became devoted to undoing what he perceived as the damage that capitalism had wrought in Latin America, especially in the overthrow of Guatemala's left-wing government in a CIA-backed coup in 1954. The situation frustrated Guevara; he felt that President Jacob Arbenz should have held on, had the people hold on, even if it necessitated violence.

In the fall of 1954, Guevara, a lifelong asthmatic who also had terrible allergies of his own, began working in the allergy division of the Mexico City General Hospital. The following June, Ñico López, a Cuban exile he knew from his work in Guatemala, introduced him to Raul Castro. With his amazing passion for overturning imperialism, corruption, exploitation, when he encountered the Castro brothers and their band of revolutionaries in the Mexican jungle in the mid-1950s, he was ready to join the cause. He essentially saw the United States as a kind of "puppet-master" that manipulated others into oppressing their own people in the interest of profits, and he saw Batista as one of the most insidious of the U.S. "puppets."

As Castro recalls, "So Raul went to Mexico, and there, through our *compañeros* who were already there, he met Che. Of course, Che wasn't Che yet; he was Ernesto Guevara, but since the Argentines are always saying *!che hombre!*, 'che' this and 'che' that, the Cubans started calling him El Che, and it stuck."

Because of their similar backgrounds and ideals, Fidel and Che bonded quickly and easily. They were not countrymen, but they shared a political connection that transcended nationalism. As Castro explains, "[Che] was already a Marxist. Although he wasn't a member of any party at that time, he was, at that point, a Marxist by conviction . . . I was a utopian Marxist. That explains to a degree my bonding with Che. The congruence of so many ideas was perhaps one of the things that aided that bonding."

Che didn't need a lot of convincing to join the revolution. As Castro related, "He knew that in our movement there were even some *petit-bourgeois* members and a bit of everything. But he saw that we were going to fight a revolution of national liberation, an anti-imperialist revolution; he didn't yet see a socialist revolution, but that was no obstacle—he joined right up, he immediately signed on."

Che became the medic for the troops, and over the course of the training, began rising in the ranks. When it was time to board the *Granma* and head back to Cuba, Che was already easily second-in-command. In his training, the athletic Che excelled. In learning theory, he was apt. But the thing that perhaps impressed Fidel the most about Che was his fierce determination:

"Near Mexico City, there's a volcano, Popocatepetl, and every weekend, Che would try to climb Popocatepetl . . . He'd make a tremendous effort but he'd never make it to the top. The asthma prevented him. The next week, he'd try again to climb Popo, as he called it, but he wouldn't make it. He never made it to the top . . . But he kept trying to climb the mountain, and he'd have spent his entire life trying to climb Popocatepetl. He made a heroic effort, although he never managed to reach that summit. So there you see his strength of character. That gives you some idea of his spiritual strength, his constancy."

As a commander, Che was mostly respected by his troops, although there was resentment among some that he was not Cuban. Fidel brushed this off. For him, what mattered about Che was not the nation of his birth, but his qualities. "Here, in our war, he was the medic, but because of his bravery, his qualities, we gave him the command of a column, and he distinguished himself in so many ways, through so many fine qualities."

But he wasn't perfect, by any means. While Fidel found him brave, he also thought Che pushed too far, and had to reel him in often from taking too many risks with his men. Che was also righteous and outspoken, and didn't necessarily "put a cork in it" at the times it was necessary to simply keep quiet. Castro recalls a time when they were under arrest in Mexico City and Che almost got them shut down. "When did he create a problem for us? When they interrogated him and asked him, 'Are you a communist?' 'Yes I'm a communist,' he answered. And the newspapers over there in Mexico started reporting that were were a communist organization, that we were conspiring to 'liquidate democracy on the continent [South America]' and I don't know what else."

While it bothered some Cubans that this Argentine was leading them to take back Cuba, it never mattered to Che that he was fighting a battle for another country. For him, again, the fight wasn't about nationalism; it was about the fight. It was about working toward a cause that was not just a benefit for Cuba, but a possible benefit for the world. Though Castro recalls he did have at least one thing to say about it. "He said just one thing to me: 'The only thing I ask is that when the Revolution triumphs in Cuba, you not forbid me, for reasons of state, from going to Argentina to make a revolution there.'"

Che would not lead a revolution in Argentina, however. After helping Castro and company take back Cuba, he stayed with them several more years, taking on various jobs in the new government, including in land and bank reform and literacy. He eventually left Cuba to pursue other interests, including the cause of the Congo, as well as the stubborn fixation he had with Bolivia, which Castro felt he was being impatient about and tried to distract him with other causes until the time was right. It's hard to know if Che and his men would still have been executed in Bolivia in 1967 had Che listened to Castro and taken a step back.

Castro said of Che, "Che was a man who fought to the last bullet, and who had no fear of death."

CHAPTER TWELVE

THE GRANMA LANDING

"We didn't know much about sailing, and when we loaded eighty-two men, plus weapons, munitions, food and extra fuel into the Granma, it slowed the boat down tremendously, so it took seven days for the trip instead of five, and there [were] only a few inches of fuel left in the tanks. It took us two days longer than planned. And we were attacked three days after we landed."

Fully trained and ready to take down Batista, the only thing missing was a way to get the soldiers from Mexico to Cuba. They knew they needed a boat, and tried to purchase a military vessel, but to no avail. What they ended up getting instead was an old, broken-down, 43-foot yacht meant designed to accommodate 12 passengers but maybe comfortably hold 20. They had four times that many to transport through the Gulf of Mexico.

Quietly, on November 25, 1956, the crew set out on their 1,200-mile trek to save Cuba. The time was right, according to the plan, but it wasn't the best time to cross the Gulf of Mexico. It was hurricane season, and while the crew, which consisted of Fidel, Raul, Che, and most of the others (about 50 had to be left behind because there wasn't room on the boat), were lucky in that they didn't get hit with any hurricanes, the seas were still stormy.

It wasn't just the weather that wore them down those seven days at sea. There was never enough to eat and no space to lie down. The fact that it wasn't smooth sailing meant many of the men got sick, and just had to suffer it out. There was no seasickness medicine. There was very little of anything.

The boat itself was a mess. There definitely seemed a reason it was called "Granma"—it was old and falling apart. Truly an $18,000 wreck. The engines didn't work properly. There was a crack somewhere in the boat; perhaps it had cracked under all the weight it was bearing. When the men weren't throwing up over the side, they were bailing water out of the hull. Later, the boat would become an important symbol. It would be preserved and displayed, and the name "Granma" would grace provinces and newspapers and parks. But at this time, it was, well, hell on keels.

Finally, the crew arrived at Cuba, on December 2, 1956, undetected, or so they thought. They grounded the boat in the swamp, about 15 miles off their intended target, and headed for the mountains, where they could be safe and begin making contact with supporters. Three days into their journey, they had found a spot that seemed like a good resting place, where they could try to regain their strength. "Some of the *compañeros* were totally exhausted," Castro recalled. "I decided to camp on a little hill with smooth, soft soil a few yards from a field of sugar cane that you could chew and suck on. The men spread out with their platoons to rest and wait for night to come on."

Butt the spot they chose was about 100 yards from an army post—Batista's army post. Within hours, planes began flying overhead and soon enough, shots were fired at the rebels, but not from the planes—from the ground.

The men scattered. Many were killed. They broke into smaller groups that had to work together to survive. Castro himself was left with two men who had stayed relatively close to the field, as he had. "The three of us who were hunkered down in the sugar cane waited for night to fall—it wouldn't be long—and then we headed for those big woods. There, we slept as best we could. Total forces: three men. Total weapons: my rifle with 90 rounds and Universo's with 30. That was all that was left of my command."

It was true. As far as he knew, his brother Raul and Che had both gone down. There was no way to communicate with any of the other soldiers. It was Castro and these two men, and his mind was a mess. He wasn't thinking clearly. "It's not hard to imagine what a terrible state of mind I was in after seeing all the work we'd been doing for two years go up in smoke in a question of minutes," he said.

He wasn't making the decisions, wasn't standing firm on decisions he could make, and their chance of survival seemed fleeting with each passing minute, and each encounter with the enemy. He recalls hiding out with his two men, Universo and Faustino, and the terror that never left them: "[The soldiers] could not know who the men were out in that field. But whoever they were, they attacked them with everything they had. All that happened a little after midday—I don't know the exact time. But I do know that we were underneath those leaves and straw, because they kept circling overhead in those little spotter planes all the time, watching the area. Under the sugar cane, lying there like that, the exhaustion from all the tension you've lived through for days and days just comes over you."

Those days, as he struggled to make it to the mountains with Universo and Faustino, were some of the worst he has ever lived, including the events of the Moncada attack. Not only was he living in near-certainty that he would never make it to the mountains, but all he had devoted his life to over the past couple of years and had been building to for at least a decade was crumbling to dust. He had very little hope that things would right themselves again. "Under those circumstances, what did I do? When I realized there was no way I could stay awake, that I was sure to fall asleep, I lay down on my side and put the rifle butt between my legs and the end of the barrel under my chin. I didn't want to be captured alive if the enemy should come upon me while I was asleep."

It didn't come to that. Fidel, along with both Universo and Faustino, finally made it to the camp at Sierra Maestra where some of the others waited—though not many of the others. While Che and Raul survived, and would in time make their way to the group, in total, less than 20 made it. Within days, this small group of men, now Castro's most trusted inner circle, would use their wits and whatever weapons they could scavenge to bring down Batista and his army.

CHAPTER THIRTEEN

THE TAKEDOWN

"We started organizing with two rifles. Raul, on the other hand, met us two weeks later with five guns. With the two we had, that meant we had seven. And that's when I said, for the first time, 'Now we can win this war.'"

Once reunited with his soldiers, with Raul and Che, Fidel felt he had the ground back beneath him. Evading Batista's army, armed with just one rifle and hiding with only two out of what had been 80 men—and originally more than 100 men, many of whom had to be left behind in Mexico because everyone couldn't fit on the *Granma*, Fidel had allowed himself, if only briefly, to believe that all was lost. That the battle being waged was hopeless. That perhaps it had all been a mistake.

He was happy to be reunited with his men in the Sierra Maestra, but their lack of weaponry was frustrating, to say the least, especially considering how much work had gone into training with those weapons, and how much work Fidel himself had done getting them ready. Castro said, "On the *Granma*, I calibrated those 55 rifles for accuracy at 600 meters, over 650 yards. We have three makes of rifles, and each of them had a different variation, depending on the steel and the bullet, and on the *Granma*, at a distance of 10 yeards and with a geometric formula, I calibrated all the weapons. I spent over two days calibrating those rifles."

But even stripped down to the skeleton crew they had left, less than 20 men, a quarter of their original battalion, and even left with a small number of weapons, Fidel once again had hope. Of course, strategy changes were now necessary. Castro recalled, "If we'd landed with 82 men in the right place, the place we'd planned to land at, the war might have lasted just seven months. Why? Because of experience. With those men and the experience we had, 55 weapons with telescopic sights, excellent marksmen, the war would not have lasted seven months."

Eventually they secured more weapons and even more men. So their efforts were divided between re-strategizing and re-training, along with the actual fighting of Batista's men. But again, things were moving more slowly than had been anticipated, and there would be issues aside from these that got in the way.

One of these things was Che's asthma. A lifelong sufferer of the respiratory condition, Dr. Che was not usually without his inhaler, though at one point he had gone to battle and left it behind, and this had become an issue for him when he came down with an asthma attack. It was bad for Che, but it was bad for everyone. Fidel recalled, "Our march was dangerously slowed down to a severe attack of asthma that suddenly overcame Che. At that point, he could hardly walk. We had to climb a steep mountainside; we were making our way up the incline toward a wooded area when a column of about 300 soldiers was swinging around our left flank . . . Despite the shooting, we continued up the hill, practically dragging Che, trying to reach the wooded area before the enemy column."

While some may feel Fidel is a ruthless dictator who stopped at nothing to seize and maintain power, his humanity is hard to mistake when it came to his men, and especially when it came to Che. Fidel was not one to leave men behind. On the *Granma* voyage, there had reputedly been a man that fell overboard. Precious time and fuel were expended to try to retrieve him; and after hours spent, they finally pulled him back into the boat. It's unknown whether this soldier survived once they landed in Cuba. The important thing to note, though, is that they would have landed in Cuba earlier, and there would have been more room on the boat! But Castro did not leave men behind.

But eventually, Che's asthma was overwhelming them all, Che especially. He really could not go on. So Fidel made arrangements to keep him safe and have medication sent. He then was forced to forge on without him, at least temporarily. Soon Che would get his medication and would be back on his feet, leading his own men again.

Even with a smaller crew and less than half their original weapons count, Fidel and his men fought strong and, more importantly, smart. Instead of relying on massive numbers of troops to overcome Batista's men, they had to make the most of what they had. They mastered the art of the ambush, and used tricks to surprise the other army, throwing them off their game, and to great success. It was amazing. Castro explained, "After the first combat we set up an ambush for those paratroopers; by now we had almost 30 men, as I said. There were no casualties in the first combat, none in the second. As a doctor, Che had nothing to do."

As the months went on, they had some casualties, naturally, but their numbers continued to grow. Still, Fidel felt for the fallen. He said, "In our defense against [Batista's] offensive we lost several brave, combative commanders who'd been extremely distinguished leaders."

Luckily for Fidel, it would not be during this war against Batista that he would lose Che. Fully recovered, armed with the medication he needed as well as strong men and a strong will, Che was ready not only to act, but to help the rebels win. Fidel said of one mission in particular, "Che carried out the mission I'd sent him on. The battle at Uvero lasted about three hours. The enemy had 11 dead and 19 wounded, among them the lieutenant commanding the barracks. We lost seven combatants and had eight wounded, several of them seriously. Once we'd achieved our victory, we provided aid to those who needed it. Che and the garrison doctor treated the enemy wounded, which there were more of than our own, and then they treated ours. Che treated all of them. You can't imagine that man's sensitivity." Fidel would remain impressed with Che, with his strength and sensitivity, throughout the war against Batista, and Che would prove to be not only a great doctor but an essential player in their efforts in taking down Batista.

Battles were waged, and Fidel and his men only seemed to get stronger with every one. As the months passed, Batista's troops dwindled while Fidel's force grew bigger and stronger. Fidel's men were stronger and better trained in fighting in the mountains, and they also had the ears of the locals, who were tired of oppression and thus fired up to join Castro and his crusade. From an army of barely 20 left from the rigorous training in Mexico, they grew to hundreds of soldiers and hundreds more supporters.

Batista was done. As Fidel recalled of the last attack made on them, "Once this last offensive was defeated, our forces, equipped with weapons seized by the enemy, grew from 300 to 900 armed men, and with them, we invaded practically the whole country."

They were unstoppable now, Fidel and his men. The revolution was in full effect. Fidel had taken back Cuba. Batista fled to the "safety" of the Trujillo-ruled Dominican Republic on December 31, 1958, and without Batista in command, his army ultimately folded.

The July 26th Movement was a success, though it would be days after the victory that Castro and his men would officially close the books on the battle, and a new leader would be installed to replace the dictator Fidel and his troops had finally been successful in overthrowing.

CHAPTER FOURTEEN

BATISTA FALLS

"I believe that there is no country in the world including any and all the countries under colonial domination, where economic colonization, humiliation, and exploitation were worse than in Cuba, in part owing to my country's policies during the Batista regime. I approved the proclamation which Fidel Castro made in the Sierra Maestra, when he justifiably called for justice and especially yearned to rid Cuba of corruption. I will even go further: to some extent it is as though Batista was the incarnation of a number of sins on the part of the United States. Now we shall have to pay for those sins. In the matter of the Batista regime, I am in agreement with the first Cuban revolutionaries. That is perfectly clear."
—President John Fitzgerald Kennedy, October 1963

It would be some time before JFK would be elected president of the United States, inheriting the Cuban situation from his predecessor, Dwight D. Eisenhower, but his words are fitting here as they show that what was going on in Cuba in the last part of the 1950s wasn't seen outside of Cuba as just something that was simply happening there and having no bearing on the rest of the world. It wasn't something isolated happening on a Caribbean island; it was a movement the world noticed.

JFK spoke these words in an interview some time after Fidel and his men began bringing revolution to Cuba, but it helps give a perspective to what was going on as Castro's small guerrilla army expanded in numbers and power, and began to overcome Batista's army. How was this ragtag group of guerrillas succeeding in taking down a powerful and established army? Castro said, "I always trusted the possibilities of an irregular war. Throughout history, in all wars since the times of Alexander and Hannibal, victory was always within the grasp of those who used the wiles of secret in their movements, and surprise in their deployment of men and arms, terrain, and tactics."

That was the secret: the element of surprise. It didn't matter that Batista's troops were so well trained and well armed; they were no match for the inspired strategies of Castro and they were demoralized trying to navigate and wage war in the unfamiliar jungles where most of the battles were waged. "We soon developed the art of confusing the enemy forces, to force them to do what we wanted them to do," Castro recalled.

It didn't matter that Batista's men nearly tripled Castro's *compañeros*; Castro's armies grew by the day. New weapons were amassed from every successful attack. Batista's traditional army was weakening, while impoverished Cubans were joining with Castro by the day. Castro said, "Our army grew very quickly at the end, because in December 1958, I had, according to my calculations, just 3,000 armed men, but when we seized all those weapons on 1 January 1959, our army grew within just weeks to 40,000 men. But the war was won, in less than two years, by 3,000 men. One mustn't forget the time [it took]." Or, more like how little time it took, all things considered.

The fact that Castro and his army were gaining support as they went was commendable, though if only the people were able to come together before the fighting began, before the revolution came, even before the Moncada attacks, things might have been different. Castro said, "If the political front that we had proposed, the union of all anti-Batista forces, had happened from the beginning, the Batista regime would have collapsed on its own accord, maybe without another drop of blood being spilled." But that was the only way it could be.

Despite what some might think of Castro and his Batista takedown, it's important to know that Castro prided himself always on fighting like a gentleman. His guerrillas had been trained to fight to win, but not to resort to any tactics that would make them seem even remotely like terrorists. They were not terrorists; they were revolutionaries. "For . . . years, since we disembarked from the *Granma*, those guidelines have been in place: no assassination, no civilian victims, no use of the methods of terror," Castro said. "Why should we have done those things? It never occurred to us."

After seven months of fighting, Castro's guerrilla army had expanded from the less than 20 soldiers who had survived the attacks since the Granma landing and swelled in number to the thousands. Batista's army was overwhelmed, and Castro arranged to meet with one of Batista's generals, Chief of the Joint Staff Eulogio Cantillo.

General Cantillo had tried to take down the guerrillas by devising strategies he'd hoped would drive them out of the jungles and bring them down to the south coast where his men, about 14 battalions with about 12,000 soldiers, would be better able to fight them. When the situation began to seem hopeless, Cantillo agreed to a meeting with Castro, and a truce was made.

Castro had thought of Cantillo as a respectable man, not like most of the savages who worked on Batista's staff. However, when Batista fled Cuba on December 31, it was clear that it had been Cantillo who had enabled Batista to leave undetected, and Castro quickly changed his mind about Cantillo. Later, during Castro's tribunals, Cantillo would be sentenced to serve 15 years in prison, for which he served a portion, then left Cuba for Miami.

Batista left Cuba on December 31, 1958; the following day, Castro declared victory. "What did we do on 1 January, 1959? Five years, five months, and five days after the attack on Moncada on July 26, 1953? Exact numbers. That's the time that had passed since the attack on Moncada, including almost two years in prison, another almost two years outside Cuba preparing for an armed return, and another two years and one month at war."

At last, victory was theirs. The government had been overthrown, the president had sneaked away, and Castro was now in control. It was time for him to make his way from the jungles of the Sierra Maestra to Havana, where change would finally start to begin. It wouldn't be easy to get there, though. Castro said, "It took me eight days to reach Havana, because at every provincial capital I had to stop and make a speech and so on—there were crowds waiting for us everywhere along the line. A tank was the only thing that could get us through—you couldn't get through in a truck or you'd be crushed."

Crowds of people wanted to embrace this new leader and his *compañeros* who had overthrown the dictator who had oppressed them, anxious to know what the future had in store for them. Would Castro and his revolution really change things for these people, or was a different kind of oppression about to govern them? That would all depend on perspective.

CHAPTER FIFTEEN

CHANGING THE GOVERNMENT

"I had no interest in being president. What I wanted to pursue was at the Revolution, the army, the development of our heroic Rebel army. I mean, an election might come along at some point and I might run, but I wasn't really thinking about that at the time."

Down with Batista, up with the people! 1959 was a brand-new year, and the people of Cuba—at least, the poorest among them—were hot with anticipation for a brand-new beginning. Gone were the years of oppression. Now was the time for all to prosper, not just the middle and especially the upper classes. But that was another story. For the peasants, a new day was about to dawn on a country that had for nearly a decade been oppressed by a tyrant who himself had been under the control of capitalist interests at any costs, including the prosperity and lives of his own people.

All that was over now; even those who remained from the old regime had to respect the way the Rebels took back the country and fell in line. It was an "irregular" war, but Castro and his *compañeros* claimed victory without crossing lines. They abided by the laws of war, and for that, they had earned respect. As Castro said,

"When an enemy comes to respect and even admire their adversary, you've won a great psychological victory. They admire you because you've managed to defeat them, because you've hit them hard but at the same time respected them, because you haven't humiliated them, you haven't insulted them, and especially because you haven't murdered."

Castro stood firm in that notion. He and his guerrilla force never acted like terrorists. They weren't traditionalists, but they played the game the right way.

Speaking of playing the game the right way, it was time to get a new government in order. To that end, Castro had to evaluate what was already in place and decide who stayed and who didn't. It's surprising that the entire government was not overturned, but Castro was smarter than that. He knew, especially in terms of having gained respect from those who had opposed him, that some of these people would be assets to him. "I was able to overlook that political disloyalty," Castro said. "There was no vanity in me whatsoever—what should and always did prevail was modesty and unity in the conduct of those who aspire to change society and the world. I employed calm and equanimity in seeking unity in very difficult circumstances."

Now that Cuba had no ruler, it was time for someone to be in charge, and naturally, because of his leading an army to overthrow Batista, most believed that Castro himself would be the one to take over. That wasn't Castro's plan, however.

At least not right away. Castro said, "I had said that I had no desire to be president—I wanted to show that I hadn't been in the struggle for personal interest. We also looked for a candidate, and we chose a magistrate who'd been against Batista, who'd actually acquitted revolutionaries who came before him in an important trial."

In fact, it was decided as early as April 1958 that this appointee, in whom Fidel had the utmost faith, would lead, but his reign would not last for long. Manuel Urrutia Lleó, a liberal Cuban lawyer and politician, had been a help to Castro in moving the revolution along in several ways. For one, in 1957, he had won a case in which he defended members of the movement who were being accused of being involved in anti-government activities. The following year, he traveled to the U.S. seeking support and managing to stop shipment of weapons to Batista and his men. Because of his actions, as well as his being an "educated liberal Christian," he was considered a good choice to lead the country, especially when it came to diplomatic relations with the rest of the world, especially the United States.

But as soon as he came to power, he started doing things the people were not crazy about, like closing brothels and halting the national lottery. The people weren't happy, and neither was Castro. The next month, Fidel was installed as prime minister, and with that took most of the power of the president. They were opposed on almost everything, including elections (Urrutia was in favor, Castro opposed) and Urrutia was becoming less significant by the day. Then, when Urrutia was accused of being frivolous with money, including purchasing a luxury villa while peasants starved, as well as speaking out against communism, the handwriting was on the wall. Just six months in, he was done when his resignation was demanded by the head of the Sugar Workers. He resigned and left for the United States.

Castro said, "The satisfaction of the struggle, pride in the struggle and its eventual success, victory, is a prize much greater than any government position, and when I said I wasn't interested in being president, I did so after great deliberation." But having been installed as prime minister almost immediately after the old regime was overturned, and ensuring that this position held as much, or, realistically, more than the position of president, it's easy to understand why folks have been dubious of Castro's intentions.

In any case, in July 1959, after Urrutia's farewell, Osvaldo Dorticós was appointed the new president. A wealthy lawyer who strongly opposed Batista, he, like Urrutia, was a friend to the movement. Already appointed minister of revolutionary laws in Castro's cabinet, he had played an important role in re-writing the laws of Cuba and had proven to Castro to be a strength and not an adversary, someone who could act as a figurehead for the nation while Castro pulled all the strings.

Dorticós handled the scene around the world, while Castro kept his focus on Cuba. It was Dorticós who represented Cuba in the Summit of Non-Aligned Nations in Belgrade, Yugoslavia, in 1961, and in Punta del Este, Uruguay, in 1962 at the Summit of the Organization of American States. Most significantly, it was Dorticós who gave the historic, fear-inducing speech at the UN that Cuba was in possession of nuclear weapons, and hoped never to use them. But that's another story . . .

For the next nearly 15 years, Castro and Doriticos would rule together, with Castro firmly in charge of things. It wasn't until 1976, when Castro implemented the new Cuban constitution, that Castro would become head of state and Dorticós would be demoted to president of the National Bank and a member of the Council of State, and Castro held absolute power in Cuba.

CHAPTER SIXTEEN

MILITARY TRIBUNALS

"It wasn't a Roman circus, you understand, it wasn't a basketball stadium, and that was used [against us] by the empire's publicity machine. We created tribunals that carried out our traditional trials and punished those who committed war crimes."

Castro's military tribunals were a source of controversy and was part of the reason Castro and his followers were seen in a very negative light, as violence-craving animals who didn't give fair trials and who reveled in the suffering of others. Not necessarily the case, though it was important to take action against those who had brutalized so many others. They needed to be brought to justice, for the good of the people. It had to happen, Castro said, "Because the crimes committed by Batista's thugs and henchmen, those people who thought they could get away with anything, had been horrible. And if there were no lynchings, no bloodbaths, it was because of our insistence and our promise: 'War criminals will be brought to justice and punished, as examples.'"

So, to that end, while Batista hid out in the comfy embrace

of his allies in the Dominican Republic, the people who worked for him and who followed him—hundreds of soldiers, policemen, and agents—paid for his sins, and their sins in following him. Brought up on charges that included torture and murder, these Batista supporters were publicly tried for human rights abuses and other war crimes.

Fidel and friends did not take down all Batista supporters, but the ones who were pulled down came down with great impact. For example, La Cabana Fortress, an 18th-century fortress complex on the Harbor in Havana, was taken over by rebel forces in January 1959, and Che Guevara took charge for roughly six months of what was to now act as a military prison. Here, war criminals, informants, and others were tried and executed.

While Raul Castro was third-in-command, and had been since Che came on board and worked his way to becoming second-in-command, displacing Raul, Raul had not had a lot of victories to claim in battle. But in Santiago, he made his mark. There, Raul Castro and his men seized the city, along with more than 70 of Batista's men. The men were first captured and kept as POWs, and then, at Fidel's behest and Raul's command, were publicly executed.

So some were tried and convicted and executed, and some never even got a trial to begin with. Even when there were trials, however, there was controversy.

It wasn't so much that these trials were taking place that was the issue, however. It was the way it was happening. Castro pointed out that the methods were not unusual under the circumstance: "No one says that this may have been the only revolution in which the main war criminals were tried and brought to justice, the only revolution that didn't rob or steal, didn't drag people through the streets, didn't take revenge, didn't take justice into its own hands. No one was ever lynched here. Not that some people wouldn't have liked to."

In fact, many were not tried at all, nor executed. Many of Batista's men had actually been spared. Some were permitted to simply leave the country; others were exiled as military attaches. Yet others were allowed not only to stay, but were also given positions in the new regime, as pointed out in the previous chapter.

Perhaps the biggest issue with the tribunals was the public nature of what was going on—that all these punishments for horrors were, in fact, horrors in and of themselves. The first trials were organized and put on at the Sports Palace stadium before an audience of 17,000 spectators. Castro said: "I think the error may have been in the manner, shall we say, that those trials were conducted, using public places and allowing the proceedings to be attended by a great number of our countrymen who were justly outraged by the thousands of crimes that had been committed. That might be in conflict, and in fact was in conflict, without our ideas of justice."

Many of the trials were carried out in a baseball stadium and anyone off the street could just come in and watch the action. Thousands of people crowded in to see justice done to their persecutors. That it had become a spectacle instead of a vehicle of justice was the crux of the criticism, or so Castro believed. "[The way the trials went over] was very much exploited in the United States. We lost no time in rectifying what was unquestionably a mistake. But those guilty of genocide were tried and punished according to laws that had been passed down long before the Revolution, during the war. We don't regret having done it, although I do feel pity when I remember how bitter it must have been for [the accused] to experience the hatred that the people quite rightly felt for them because of their repugnant crimes."

As all this was going on, Castro knew it wasn't going to last, and he knew the people, revenge-obsessed and bloodthirsty as they seemed, could not maintain this frenzied height of delight in the ghoulish punishments of their persecutors for long. As Castro related, "Thugs who commit monstrous crimes anywhere, almost everybody thinks should be severely punished, but when the time comes and the [criminal] is sentenced and is about to be executed, there are people who react with sadness and even with pity." It was time to wrap it up.

Eventually, the tribunals ended, and it was time to re-shape and restructure the government into something that Castro believed would truly benefit the people. Not all the people felt this way, however. As mentioned earlier, many in the upper and middle classes fled Cuba, not wanting to live in Castro's Cuba, and feeling like it wouldn't be long until he was overthrown by another uprising, and they could return. Many, if not most, of these Cubans never returned.

CHAPTER SEVENTEEN

RELIGION, RACE, & REVOLUTION

"I never saw a contradiction between the ideas that sustain me and the ideas of that symbol, of that extraordinary figure, Jesus Christ."

Two hot-button topics that arise in regards to Castro's Revolution are religion and race. Were Castro and his men anti-religion? Was racism an issue in the Revolution, and where did Castro and his followers stand on that?

First, religion. Castro was born into a Catholic family. His mother, Lina, was very religious, and raised her children as such. The young Castro made all his sacraments, and was schooled by the Jesuits. But while he would "sort of" return to the faith later in life, religion had no place in Revolution. He was a strong believer in the division between church and state, and he felt that religious people did not have their priorities straight when it came to governing.

Castro said, "The principle was established that religious believers would not be allowed to enter into the party's ranks. Believers might be treated with every consideration and respect with regard to their political position, but they couldn't become a member of the Party. And don't think it didn't take work, years, to come to the decision that we had to open the Party's doors to religious nonbelievers."

For that, among other things, Castro was considered "godless," and many believed his Revolution was anti-religious, versus what it was in reality: areligious, like asexual. It wan't against religion; it just didn't apply religion as a factor. It was especially part of how the United States attacked him. Castro said, "It was in the interest of the government of the United States to portray the Cuban Revolution as an anti-religious revolution, based on the conflicts that occurred in the first few years and forced us to take certain measures."

But because it was such an emotional issue for such a deeply Catholic nation, he got a lot of criticism for taking action against Catholic institutions, when in fact, it was all part and parcel of the bigger picture. Castro explained, "We nationalized all education, not just the Catholic schools. This is a radical, profound revelation, those are the words I use for it, and I can justify and show why—but there was not a single priest executed . . ." Castro went on to say that this was, in fact, one of the only revolutions in which priests were not executed.

Later in life, Castro would become more flexible about religion in politics, and even come to embrace certain aspects of his own Christian upbringing. As early as 1992, he would begin referring to Cuba as secular, versus atheist. He would become interested in developing a new consciousness when it came to religious thinking, "built by adding together more than just one revolutionary thought and the best ethical and humane ideas of more than one religion, of all authentic religions . . . the sum total of the preaching of many political thinkers, of many schools and of many religions." But for the time being, religion had no place in his Revolution.

Race was another story, however. Race was part of the reason the Revolution needed to be fought, as there were no people as oppressed in Cuba as much as the blacks of the nation were oppressed. Castro spoke out regularly against racism, explaining that, "For us revolutionaries, fighting racial discrimination has been a sacred principle."

A little background on blacks in Cuba. During the slave trade, roughly 900,000 Africans were brought to Cuba, versus approximately 470,000 to what is now the United States—about twice as many. The population of Cuba during the Revolution and now reflects that, with blacks making up approximately 40 percent of the population. So they are barely a minority. Yet racism, especially pre-Revolution, had been rabid, and it was a huge fighting principle for Castro and his revolutionaries. He explained, "Scientific research has tried to show what the differences are between the various ethnic groups, and it hasn't come up with anything, except little things that have nothing to do whatsoever with talent. Science has come to the aid of those who fight against racism. Yet while science has incontestably shown the true intellectual equality of all human beings, discrimination still exists."

So reradicating racism was one of the objectives of the Revolution. With the equality Castro and company fought so hard to instill, there could be no racism because all Cubans would be equal. Right? Not really. The effects did not impact racism as much as he would have liked, Castro said. "The Revolution, over and above the rights and guarantees achieved for all its citizens of whatever ethnic background or origin, has not had the same success in its fight to eradicate the differences in social and financial statuses for the black population of the country. Blacks don't live in the best houses; you find that they still have the hardest, most physically wearing and often worst-paid jobs and that they receive much less help from their family members no longer in Cuba, in dollars, than their white compatriots."

Castro had worked for decades to overturn racism in Cuba, but even today, with the population of blacks teetering over 50 percent, there are still issues. Castro said, "At the time we were naive enough to believe that decreeing total and absolute equality under the law would put an end to discrimination. Because there are two types of discrimination—one is subjective and the other is objective." It was this subjective discrimination that Castro still rallied against more than forty years after the fight began. While the election of Barack Obama as president of the United States started to change opinions, there was still much work to be done.

One of the main cause-and-effect issues Castro sees with regard to racism is that it promulgates crime. While there is racism, there is less opportunity for education for blacks. and while blacks are less educated, they are more inclined towards criminal activity. Castro explained, "You'd be amazed if you saw how many young people between 20 and 30 years old—and we're doing further research on this—are in prison, where, despite the enormous number of professionals and intellectuals in this country, only 2 percent of those in prison are the children of professionals and intellectuals." His point was that the more educational opportunities there are for blacks, the more inclined they will be to pursue professions like law and medicine, and the less likely they will end up behind bars having committed petty—and not so petty—crimes to try to survive.

Castro said, "We have discovered that there is an inverse relation between knowledge, culture, and crime; for example, the greater the knowledge, culture, and access to university education, the less crime."

CHAPTER EIGHTEEN

CASTRO'S SOCIAL REFORM

"At the time, no one believed in any program put forth by any Cuban revolutionary, because lots of them had put forth programs and none of them had followed through on them, Our problem, actually, was that we over-followed through on them."

While it has been widely believed that the Revolution to socialize Cuba meant the wealthy were taken down by force and thrown out of their homes and out of the country by the poor and the oppressed, this was not the case, according to Castro. No one was expelled; people, mainly people of the upper and upper-middle classes, chose to leave, believing they would return when action was taken against these seemingly "lawless" band of guerrillas, and when everything was restored to normal, they could go home again. But nothing in their idea of what was "normal" was ever going to be normal again.

There is valid reason for speculation. In 1959, the creation of the Ministry for the Recovery of Misappropriated Assets did spark a seizure of properties. "[In May 1959] we created the Agrarian Reform Laws, the first of which we passed on 17 May that year," Castro said. Farms were taken over by the government, and industry was nationalized. This affected the holdings of private citizens of Cuba as well as foreign interests. Castro said, "We even issued an administrative order: 'The law will recognize no right to land taken by persons through their own means.' [Because of this] there was going to be total chaos within a revolution that had the support of more than 90 percent of the population, according to the surveys. Because there were rivalries and disagreements and all that sort of thing."

By August 1960, more than $25 billion worth of property and industry had been nationalized. Castro didn't miss those who opposed his ideas and left the country because they were against his process, and has referred to these defectors as "enemies" at certain times.

It was clear that Castro was ready for big sweeping change, and be believed the people of Cuba, all the people of Cuba, supported him in that. He said, "There was a kind of *de facto* amnesty, on behalf of unity. Everyone accepted the decision made by the 26th of July Movement and the Rebel army for the sake of unity among all those who to a greater or lesser extent had fought against the tyranny."

Those who opposed him simply left. "[M]any of those who went to Miami . . . were not actually planning to take part in bringing down the Revolution," Castro explained. "They all lived under the conviction that it would be the United States and its powerful armed forces that would bring down the

Revolution. Many of the rich and privileged who left Cuba and abandoned their homes and abandoned everything—it's not that we expelled them or took their homes away. They said, 'This will last four or five months. How long can a Revolution last in this country?'"

Right from the beginning, laws were created to improve the situation for blacks and women, and efforts were made to improve medical facilities, housing, communications, and education. By the end of 1960, all Cuban children were in school, versus roughly half before the Revolution. Unemployment had been drastically reduced. "We reinstated all the workers who had been fired during the Batista period, in all the factories," Castro explained. "Our accounts weren't particularly 'economics-based,' and they didn't jibe very well with the ideas put forth by . . . what we today call the 'pro-Yankee neo-liberals,'" but the fact remains that people went back to work. More people working meant less crime and less corruption, and there was also reform for how people lived. "We also drastically reduced rents, which later became a new rent-reform that turned renters into buyers of real estate," Castro said.

In addition to the improvements being made on the ground level for society, attention was paid to the cultural aspects that had been neglected, as is wont to happen in a society that consists mainly of people working and over-working to just get food on the table. Now that those concerns had been addressed, more attention could be paid to enhancing quality of life.

There were still those who remained who did not support Castro and his actions, however; Castro did not turn a blind eye to these groups. Rather, he established the Committees for Defense of the Revolution in September 1960, which was designed to monitor suspicious behaviors and communication, and deal with anyone who looked to be acting against the Revolution. Castro felt this necessary as no one would have rebelled against what was going on if they understood what was going on. Castro said, "There was widespread ignorance about economics and what prevailed were the old slogans and bywords of unions and campesino organizations, all very justifiable, but all within the framework of a capitalist society that had to be transformed."

It's important to grasp that while Fidel was forcing through all this power, he, was not technically in charge. The title of president belonged to the Castro-appointed Urrutia, though Castro had become prime minister in 1959. It wasn't long before he saw that some of the cooperation, or, rather, lack of cooperation, was coming from inside the government, and from powerful places.

Castro explained, "We had to act in the face of idiocies, stupidities. Every few minutes there was a problem because, for example, Urrutia said, with no waning, that all the casinos had to be closed—there was still gambling and that sort of thing—and the reaction to that was pretty strong on the part of the people who worked in the casinos and tourism and so on." Castro wanted to disempower and also empower the people at once. He wanted the government to control all the financial interests in the country, but he wanted the citizens to feel in some way in control of their personal interests, and taking away the casinos definitely stood in the way of that.

Castro would also take action to have Cuban not be dependent in any way on the United States, who he felt worked against him and did whatever was possible to punish him and the Revolution. He was determined to create Cuba into a world power that could thrive without capitalism and poison capitalist thinking.

He was very concerned with the plight of the poor, and worked to make these people self-sufficient, so to speak. First they had to collect all the land they could; then it was time to dole it out. As he explained, "Later we worked hard to establish agricultural cooperatives. We also favored state agricultural cooperation because those enormous tracts of land . . . how could we divide all that land up and distribute it . . . ?"

Other social reforms in the works included those to empower races and disempower religion. He abolished private clubs and declared Cuba to be a one-party socialist state on May 1, 1961. He instated free health care and education through high school.

Castro also set forth social reform for women, which has been one of the more controversial aspects of his reform. While many believe he made incredible advances for women, about as many believe that there has never been a more oppressive society for women than the Cuban nation under Castro's rule. People have many opinions, and there seems to be evidence to support both sides, but the truth remains a mystery.

CHAPTER NINETEEN
CASTRO AND WOMEN'S REFORM

"I organized a unit of women in the Sierra, the Marianas. We showed that women could be as good at soldiering as men. I had to fight hard against machismo there, because we had . . . the lightest weapons reserved for the women, and some men said, 'How can we give a woman an M-I?'—this was after Batista's last offensive—'Why don't I get one?' I had a phrase I used with some of the men—I'll tell you what it was. I'd say, 'Listen, you know why [we're using women]? I'll tell you—because they're better soldiers than you are."

The topic of women, of Castro's relationship with women, treatment of women, regard for women, respect for women, courts a fair amount of controversy for those who study his life and career. There are as many texts to support that he respects and supports women as there are articles and other documented evidence that Castro's Cuba is an exploitative, torturous environment that oppresses women worse than any

Third World regime. Which is correct?

It's known that while Castro had an arm's-length relationship with his father, he and his mother, Lina Ruz Gonzalez, enjoyed a warm, even close, relationship. When Castro was in prison after being captured and tried for storming the Moncada Barracks, Lina, his mother had visited him more than once in prison, and offered her support for his efforts. Not much is known about her and their relationship after Castro came to power; the details of Castro's personal life are generally off-limits unless he chose to share them. What is known, however, is that despite that he was acting in the interests of the poor, and not in the interests of their class, she stood behind her son.

While in college, Fidel married Mirta Diaz-Balart, and the marriage did not end well, mainly due to her loyalties not lying where he believed they should be; that even if she and their son were starving to death while he served out his jail sentence, not only was she to stand by him, she was not to accept help from her family.

Not only was this marriage fairly short-lived, but it was marred by Fidel's many alleged infidelities, at least one of which had been confirmed when a letter intended for his mistress landed in his wife's hands. That ended with a bitter custody battle, forged and won by Fidel in his cell. Mirta remarried, leaving their son behind in Cuba.

Fidel would marry again, but not before having multiple affairs and fathering several illegitimate children with them. In fact, Fidel would continue to enjoy a string of lovers, reportedly throughout his life. Several years ago, the *New York Post* published an article about known men who have had the most lovers. Among the names on the list were Warren Beatty and Jack Nicholson, both known for their dalliances. Topping the list, however, by tens of thousands ahead of the rest, was Fidel Castro, having had a reported 35,000 women in his bed. Whether this is number is accurate or not has not been confirmed by Fidel; though close advisors have confirmed that Fidel generally takes a woman for lunch and dinner, and apparently also breakfast sometimes.

His womanizing aside, however, it's important to note that he has placed women in positions of importance. During the Revolution, Celia Sanchez was as important as Che or Raul. Reportedly, anyone who wanted to discuss anything with Fidel had to go through her.

During the attacks on the Moncada Barracks, he relied heavily on women, who fought right alongside the men, including Haydee Santamaría, who, in prison following their capture, had been served her brother's eyeballs as proof of his demise; and Melba Hernández, in whose apartment the plans for the attack were laid out and discussed. Fidel has never taken away from their contribution to his cause.

After the Revolution, Castro made certain women's rights part of the forefront of his program of social reform, including creating a generous maternity situation for women. Castro said, "Since women also have childbirth as a natural function we give them, if they have children, a year off to raise their baby—not to encourage them to have more children, but the best thing that can happen to a child when he comes into the world is to have his mother's influence, and his mother's milk."

After the Revolution, the Rebel Government established the Federation of Cuban Women for the advancement of women in Cuba, and Cuban women have the same constitutional rights as men, and are constitutionally guaranteed the same opportunities as men. They also, at the time of this writing, hold 48.9 percent of the seats in Parliament—a far cry from the percentage of women in the United States who hold office. They do, however, struggle to make as earn as men, like in the U.S., though Castro seemed determined to fix that.

All of this is well and good, except there's a darker side of the story of women in Cuba and the way they are treated, though the research seems to indicate that this is not at the hands of the government, but of splinter groups.

Fidel said, "Today we might say that we are the least *machista* country, not in the world, I wouldn't say that, but at least in this hemisphere. We have created a culture of equality and respect, which you're aware is not something you find in all of our societies . . . [O]ur machismo was inherited and we know very well how all that was inherited and cultivated in capitalist societies . . . My own feelings were different . . . I had a feeling of solidarity, because I saw and suffered over the way women were discriminated against in that exploitative society."

CHAPTER TWENTY

CASTRO MEETS WORLD

"[I]n the first few days and months those terrorist activities were organized by Batista elements, really —former police officers and Batista people mixed in with some counter-revolutionaries. But even then, the U.S. administration, using those elements, was working intensely against Cuba. In the months prior to the invasion of 66, the CIA was frantically creating anti-Cuba and counter-revolutionary organizations—over time it created more than 300 of them. And today we know that in March 1960 President Eisenhower signed an order authorizing a 'powerful propaganda offensive' against the Revolution and a clandestine plan of action to topple the Cuban government."

Fidel Castro has always had a lot to say about the United States being against Cuba, going on well before the success of the Cuban Revolution and its various reforms in the late 1950s and early 1960s; well before the attacks on the Moncada Barracks in the early 1950s. Between Batista's two reigns of Cuba, once in the 1940s and then his forcible takeover in the

1950s, Batista lived in the United States, where he picked up all his capitalist notions and made relationships that he would later work to nurture, even at the cost of exploiting his own people. That, for Castro, was the biggest outrage: that one could turn his back on the interests of his own countrymen to make money for those who had even less interest in the welfare of the people.

The United States was where Batista got his ideas; the United States had encouraged, even empowered, Batista to carry them out in Cuba. Batista had to go, along with all his alliances. Batista had made Cuba dependent on the source of its exploitation, and Castro worked tirelessly to put an end to that.

To that end, though, Castro knew the story wasn't one-sided. He knew that for as hard as he pulled away from the controlling capitalism of the United States, there would be pushback. Whether it was all valid or not was irrelevant to Castro; he believed it, and that was all that mattered. He believed that the United States was actively terrorizing Cuba.

"Sabotage, the infiltration of men and the draining of military equipment in order to sabotage us and encourage uprising and terrorist activities."

"They sent in planes to spray the cane fields with incendiary materials . . . They hijacked our airplanes and flew them to the U.S., and many of those planes were destroyed, others confiscated."

"They killed diplomats, they killed our *compañeros*, even in the U.S."

Several months after the Cuban Revolution, Castro made a visit to the United States, the first since his ill-fated Miami honeymoon in the 1940s—the trip during which he lost all his money. During his 11-day trip, for which he had not been given or accepted formal government invitation, he was the consummate tourist. He caught a game at Yankee Stadium, he visited the Bronx Zoo, and he placed a wreath on the tomb of George Washington. He wished to meet with then-president Dwight D. Eisenhower, but Eisenhower refused, sending Vice President Richard Nixon instead. The insult did not go unheeded, the meeting did not go that well, and the visit went downhill from there.

Castro spoke before the Council on Foreign Relations, describing in great detail why Cuba would not be dependent on the U.S. His statements were greeted with great heckling from the Americans present. It was a frustrating waste of time that ended with Castro storming out. Castro said, "From the first moment [to this day], the American administration has been working to create an unfavorable image of the Cuban Revolution. They have carried out huge publicity campaigns against us, huge attempts to isolate Cuba. The objective has been to halt the influence of revolutionary ideas. They broke off diplomatic relations in the 1960s and took measures to impose an economic blockade." Two years later, nearly to the day, would come the Bay of Pigs invasion.

Perhaps the most insidious conspiracy Castro believes to have been a device of the United States against the Cuban people was the so-called "Operation Peter Pan," in which 14,000 children were exiled from Cuba, separated from their families, never to be reunited. Castro explained, ". . . Operation Peter Pan, the kidnapping, practically, of 14,000 of this country's children, after our adversaries invented the appalling lie that the Revolution was going to take children away from their parents, take away the parents' custody.

Under that pretext, or due to that unfounded or absurd fear, 14,000 of this country's children were clandestinely sent to the United States, and several Catholic priests who were opposed to the Revolution took part in that kidnapping, as did Catholic priests in Miami."

So, in Castro's eyes, it was the U.S. government that scared the Cuban people into tossing their children into the "better" capitalist abyss—a misguided attempt to try to "rescue" them from great evils, a horrible conspiracy sparked by the United States to weaken Cuba and hit the people in a place they could not ignore. The rumor was that the government was going to take children away from their parents; that like everything else that had been nationalized, so, too, would parenting.

Castro said, "When you're dealing with things involving such deep emotions, people go crazy. They're easily taken in because of the kind of lie it is, the circumstances of the moment, and the way the lie is spread. In this case, given an emotion such as the emotion of parenthood, that mad idea hit a nerve, it hit people's instinct—they couldn't process it. Which is why [our enemies] were able to scare even so many middle-class parents, and that made the exodus, the clandestine shipment of the children, much easier and many families were separated forever."

There was more to it; in fact, the more it went on, the more insidious the fate of these children became. Castro had later quipped, "It's been 46 years and we still don't have enough facilities for the mothers who want to send their children to childcare centers." In other words, how could the people really believe that the government was going to be able to care for all of these children?

The answer was more horrific than anything that could be

imagined. It was so horrific, in fact, it could only be imagined, but the people, described in essence by Castro as fearful and ignorant and misguided, believed it could be true. "[The Americans] said we were going to turn the children into tinned meat," he says. "That we were going to send them off to the Soviet Union, and in the Soviet Union they were going to be turned into tinned meat and sent back here in in tins . . . It's pure fantasy, although that didn't keep it from being believed—it was believed because those lies were associated with the most powerful human instinct. The instinct of a mother or father, especially a mother's."

These conspiracies mentioned here are only the tip of the iceberg of how Castro feels the United States worked against him. Conspiracies, including the 600-plus assassination attempts Castro believes the CIA, the United States, have made on his life, could be a book in and of itself. Suffice to say, Castro knew who his allies were, notably the USSR, and who they were not (the U.S.), and that understanding would lay the foundation for the Bay of Pigs invasion and the subsequent Cuban Missile Crisis.

To this day, Castro resents the U.S. government in turning his people against him, and believes the children who were exiled in Operation Peter Pan, now grown, resent it too. He said, "Many of them are adults now and they criticize their parents. Up there in Miami there was no place to house them . . . a mass of parentless Cuban children scattered all over the United States." He believes they would have had a much better life had the U.S. not gotten involved; the U.S., of course, believes differently.

CHAPTER TWENTY-ONE

CASTRO AND KHRUSHCHEV

"Although it wasn't calculated that way, the support of the USSR was essential after the triumph of 1959. We wouldn't have had that support in 1953. In 1953, the spirit and policy of Stalin prevailed in the USSR. Although Stalin had died a few months earlier, in March 1952, it was still the same 'Stalin era' . . . And Khrushchev was not Stalin."

Castro was smart enough to know that it was a good idea for a small country like Cuba to align itself with a world power. The United States, while in close proximity, was not going to be that power. Cuba needed to align with a power that shared their ideals, would protect their interests, and which could also be an economic outlet for them. The Soviet Union was the logical choice.

Nikita Khrushchev was just the leader to align their interests with, though Khrushchev and the Soviet Union in general didn't have much of an understanding of the Cuban

Revolution and what Castro and his *compañeros* were trying to accomplish at the time. In fact, initially, Khrushchev had been misinformed that Castro was working for the CIA—not a person Khrushchev would choose to be involved with. However, after sending an ambassador to Cuba in February 1960, Anastas Mikoyan, Khrushchev learned that Cuba did share interests with the USSR, and could use their help.

Because Cuba had been embargoed by the U.S., they needed help economically, and Khrushchev decided it would be okay to begin a trade with Cuba, fuel from the USSR in exchange for sugar from Cuba. It was meant to be a temporary measure, but continued and kept the Cubans economically solvent for years to come. But soon the relationship would become political, and create chaos between the USSR and the U.S. Castro remained diplomatic. In a letter to Khrushchev, he wrote, "I convey to you once again the infinite gratitude of the Cuban people to the Soviet people, who have been so generous and fraternal with us, and our profound gratitude and admiration to you [personally], as well as our desires for success in the enormous task and grave responsibilities that you have in your hands."

The Bay of Pigs invasion in April 1961 would force Khrushchev's hand to make a commitment to Cuba beyond original expectation—one that would stress relations between the U.S. and the USSR as an attack on Cuba would be seen as an attack on the USSR. For the time being, it was viable for Khrushchev, even desirable, as after the invasion, Cuba had declared itself firmly a socialist nation, and it was in the interests of the USSR to preserve this kind of thinking.

As Castro affirms in another letter to Khrushchev, explaining their defense against the U.S. "What we did in the face of the events, Comrade Khrushchev, was prepare ourselves to fight. In Cuba there was but one kind of alarm: the alarm that called our people to arms. When in our judgment the imperialist attack became imminent, I decided that I should communicate that news to you, and alert both the government and the Soviet [military] command—since there were no Soviet forces committed to fighting alongside us in defense of the Republic of Cuba against outside attack or of the possibility if an attack that it was not without power to halt, although we might indeed resist it . . ."

While Khrushchev seemed to believe standing up for Cuba was the right thing to do, that it was noble and prestigious to lend aid to their infant communist cousin, he also knew that straining relations with the U.S. over it was not going to be without ramifications, and the events of the Cuban Missile Crisis brought those fears home.

In an interview with Barbara Walters in 2002, Castro said, "Even though Nikita [Khrushchev] was a bold man, he was a courageous man . . . and I can make criticisms of him . . . of the mistakes he made. I have reflected a lot on that. . . . He misled Kennedy. That was his main . . . flaw." He also admitted he felt Khrushchev had also not been straight with Cuba. "Believe me. We were not interested in becoming part of the whole contention between the two countries. We would not have accepted the missiles if they had said that it was related to the balance of power."

In any case, following the crisis, there were "no hard feelings" between Castro and Khrushchev. In June 1963, Castro visited the Soviet Union, a visit of only 11 days versus the year before, where he'd stayed nearly five weeks, the reason for which was there was much work to be done back at home. He was given the red-carpet treatment and a 21-rifle salute, and Khrushchev announced Castro as "an example for all Latin America." Castro was bestowed a "Soviet Hero" award in a grand ceremony, a gesture of "eternal friendship," erasing any trepidation or stress between the leaders caused by the events that had taken place during the Crisis the year before.

Upon his return, Castro was glad to report that Khrushchev's people "expressed by their deeds their love for and solidarity with Cuba." During that trip, Castro was embraced as a beloved baby brother, and he and Khrushchev sat down and hammered out details for the export deals that would sustain Cuba for years to come. Castro eagerly took in all the advances the Soviets were making in agriculture, construction, and innovation, and returned to Cuba energized and eager to prove that the capitalist model wasn't the only economic model that could succeed.

CHAPTER TWENTY-TWO

TROUBLE IN PLAYA GIRÓN (THE BAY OF PIGS)

"[A]fter the battles, when people were full of adrenaline, enraged by the deaths, the men wounded, the tension of the battles, and this was during the first years of the Revolution, and many of our combatants were from the militias, volunteers who were there, laborers, campansinos and students, and there was not as much as a blow with a rifle butt. The men were returned to the United States are there, the ones who are still alive, in Miami—you can ask them to see whether there's a single one of them who'll will say he was so much as struck. There isn't a single case."

While Castro continued to spread his socialist and communist notions throughout his island country, endeavoring to spread the message to the world through all his success, his detractors, namely the U.S., were ready to stop him, and to do so, they would use some of Castro's own people—Cuban exiles who did not "drink the Kool-Aid" Castro poured,

Cubans who wanted their country back the way it had been during Batista's reign, when they had prospered.

While the attack on Playa Girón, or more commonly known, the Bay of Pigs, would occur in April 1961, two years after Castro's visit to the States, it had been in motion for almost as long as the Cuban Revolutionaries had been in power.

It started with oil. One of the first actions Castro took against the U.S. in 1960 was to order the Cuban refineries, controlled then by the U.S., to process oil from Soviet refineries. When the refineries refused, Castro nationalized them and forced them. In retaliation, the U.S. stopped importing sugar from Cuba, putting a strain on the Cuban economy. By October 1960, the U.S. government had banned all Cuban imports, creating an embargo that would last for many decades.

Cuba fought back by further nationalizing and taking over more than 500 American businesses in Cuba. The fighting continued, with U.S. Secretary of State Christian Herter, calling out Castro as "following faithfully the Bolshevik pattern" during the August 1960 meeting of the Organization of American States. Castro spat back that the poor in America were living "on the bowels of the imperialist monster." Things began escalating quickly from that point.

After the 1960 election, Eisenhower was out of office, and, in the opinion of the American people, so was Richard Nixon, who had lost a presidential run against the young and handsome John F. Kennedy. Kennedy was more respected by Castro than his predecessors, but that didn't mean the U.S. was going to change the course of its plans for Cuba. The invasion had already been set in motion, though it would not happen for several more months. Explained Castro, "Kennedy really inherited the plan from Eisenhower and his vice president, Richard Nixon. The invasion was a *fait accompli*; plans existed for destroying the Revolution, despite the fact that at that point the Revolution wasn't even socialist."

The CIA took the lead on the Castro invasion. As the threat of communism was something that weighed heavily on Americans, especially American politicians and businessmen, since the onset of the Cold War, agencies like the CIA had been set up to combat it and prevent it spreading. The CIA was the counter to the USSR's KGB.

Richard Bissell, the CIA's deputy director at the time, was put in charge of the invasion. Bissell liaised with Cuban exiles and worked to form an army of mercenaries who, in effect, would be committing treason against their own country by attacking it. The U.S. didn't want it to look like the U.S. was attacking Cuba; they wanted to make it seem like it was as an act of retaliation by exiles who wanted their country back. The plan was approved by Eisenhower in March of 1960; on August 18, he approved a budget of $13 million to fund the operation.

It was probably believed that while Eisenhower would no longer be in power, Nixon, of course, would defeat the upstart senator from Massachusetts, and that the plan would be carried out without issue, whether Eisenhower was still president or not. It was true. What was planned was already far enough along, and it had to be carried out. So on January 28, 1961, President Kennedy, a week post-inauguration, was briefed on the plan, referred to as "Operation Pluto." In April, it went into effect.

Castro said, "So then Kennedy, with reservations, put Ei-

A young Fidel Castro visits Russia in 1963.

Santiago de Cuba, the proud birthplace of Cuba's revolution.

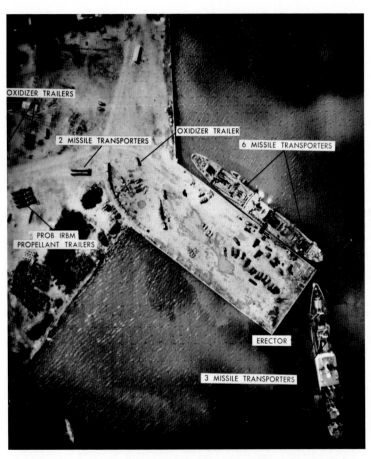

United States spy planes capture a photograph of a Soviet missile site in Cuba in 1962.

*A missile on display in Havana
commemorates the Cuban Missile Crisis.*

Cuban flags on display.

A view of Havana's Capitol building.

Old-fashioned American cars driving on the streets of Havana.

*Residents stand near damaged buildings
in the city of Havana.*

The Plaza de la Revolución in Havana is the site of many of Fidel Castro's famous speeches.

A confident-looking Fidel Castro speaks to the press in 1989.

A Fidel Castro poster and the Cuban flag adorn a building in Havana, Cuba in 2016.

Hundreds of thousands of people parade through Havana with flags and posters of Fidel Castro on International Worker's Day in 2016.

*President Castro speaks passionately
at a press conference in 1989.*

Fidel Castro's takes a tour of Uzbekistan in 1963.

In 2011, a Havana billboard displays a powerful political slogan used by Castro: "Socialism or death."

Flowers are placed outside the Cuban embassy in Moscow following Fidel Castro's death.

senhower's and Nixon's plan into effect—he believed the plan developed by the CIA and the Pentagon would have the support of the [Cuban] people, that the people would rush into the streets to welcome the invaders and that militias wouldn't fight, that they'd rise against the country's government." They even had a new leader-in-waiting, ready to take over as soon as Castro was brought down. They underestimated Castro.

On April 15, eight bombers opened fire on Cuban air fields, and on April 16, the main invasion landed on the beach of Playa Girón. They easily overcame what they perceived was the entire resistance against them. "They saw immediately what formula we'd used to bring down Batista to defeat that army, which was a combination of armed strength and popular support," Castro said. But the U.S. still underestimated their enemy.

Castro recalled, "The mercenaries had a squadron of B-26 bombers piloted by not only American crews but also officers from the former Batista air force; the planes bore the insignia of the Cuban armed forces. They launched a surprise attack on 15 April, hitting the bases used by our modest air force. This attack was the announcement that the aggression was imminent. The next day, at the burial of the victims, I proclaimed the socialist nature of our Revolution."

Castro didn't sit behind a desk and await reports from the field. He was in the field. He was among the people, fighting alongside them. It made a spectacular statement; the Americans weren't fighting. They hadn't even sent any of their people but Cubans to fight the Cubans. And here was the leader of the Revolution, physically part of the battle. "I was in several tanks at various points during those actions," he recalled, "not just one."

The next day, the true Cuban counter-attack ensued, and the invaders were overcome and captured. By April 20, they had surrendered, though Castro had no plan to hold on to these prisoners. "What were we going to do with 1,200 'heroes' in jail?" he said. "We preferred that the 1,200 so called 'heroes' be sent back home up there." He didn't want these Cuban enemies of Cuba in Cuba. He wanted to send them back to their new homeland, but not without a price.

As Castro explained, "After they'd been in prison for a short time, we demanded that the U.S. pay compensation in medical supplies and food for children. If it had happened in the U.S. they'd have sentenced them all to life in prison, if they hadn't executed no telling how many first for treason and the rest would be in jail for life. If we'd recruited 1,000 Americans to invade the United States, anybody would have understood that sentence."

There have been many rumors surrounding the treatment of prisoners with Castro, but he denies any wrongdoing at all. While a number of mercenaries had been killed due to asphyxiation during transport, Castro contends to this day that this asphyxiation had been accidental. Prisoner abuse was not, hasn't been, and wouldn't ever be part of the plan for Castro, he claimed, despite how revved up his troops may have been. ". . . After that terrible combat there as not a single case of prisoner abuse—no hitting them with rifle butts, nothing of the sort. Not a single case."

What did Cuba want in exchange for the prisoners, whom they didn't want to begin with? Castro said, "We sentenced them to pay compensation of $100,000 per prisoner, or alternatively, a prison sentence. What we wanted was payment of compensation, not because we had any need for money but rather as a recognition by the United States government of the revolutionary victory—it was almost a kind of moral punishment."

Eventually, the prisoners would be returned, but it was Castro who decided the terms. The U.S. simply went along with it. He explained, "So we were the ones who found the solution for all those mercenaries who were in prison. The U.S. government didn't have the imagination for it."

This wouldn't be the last of the skirmishes between the superpower United States and tiny island power Cuba, however. In fact, what came next made the world stand up and take notice of Cuba as a country; if not to fully respect it, then at least to fear it. Because within a matter of months, the world would believe that the tiny island power had, in their control, the power to end the world.

CHAPTER TWENTY-THREE

CUBAN MISSILE CRISIS

"You have been and are a tireless defender of peace; I understand how bitter these hours must be for you, when the results of your superhuman efforts are so seriously threatened. Until the last moment, however, we shall maintain our hope that peace may be salvaged, and we are willing and ready to contribute whatever may be within our reach [to achieve that goal] . . . I convey to you once again the infinite gratitude of the Cuban people to the Soviet people, who have been so generous and fraternal with us, and our profound gratitude and admiration to you [personally], as well as our desires for success in the enormous task and grave responsibilities that you have in your hands."
—From a letter to Khrushchev from Fidel Castro

The humiliation in the Bay of Pigs was not one the United States was going to accept lying down, and retaliation measures were soon planned. However, also going on now was a very real understanding that Cuba was not a Third-World nation that could be bullied into accepting the will of the

United States. And not only were they a force to be reckoned with on their own, they also had a "big brother" to watch their back on the "playground." And not only was the USSR behind Cuba, but also the Chinese. The Chinese *People's Daily* reported that "650,000,000 Chinese men and women were standing by the Cuban people."

The biggest fear, however, felt around the world, in West Germany and in France, was that the USSR had armed Cuba with nuclear missiles, which Castro could and would launch at whim. How did they know the Cubans had nuclear weapons? For one, the CIA, flying unauthorized in a no-fly zone, had obtained photographic evidence. Second, Cuba readily admitted their existence. And, following the CIA's failed attack on the Bay of Pigs, Cuba convinced Khrushchev to announce that "an attack on Cuba will be considered an attack on the Soviet Union."

Khrushchev complied, with reservation, but what sparked now was the very real idea that Cuba, with the help of the USSR, had the power to end it all. Castro was not sorry; he was empowered. "The world was on the verge of thermonuclear war as a consequence of the United States's aggressively brutal policy against Cuba—a plan, approved about 10 months after the disastrous defeat they suffered in Girón and about eight months before the crisis broke out, to invade the island with the direct use of that country's naval, air, and armed forces."

How did Cuba know that another attack was being planned against them? Khrushchev again. "The Soviets managed to obtain absolutely trustworthy information about that plan, and they notified Cuba of the existence of the danger, although they weren't totally explicit—the truth is, they protected their source."

Let's backtrack a bit to understand why the world even initially suspected Cuba had missiles, their relationship to the USSR notwithstanding. When Kennedy ran for election in 1960, one of his major platforms was missile gaps, meaning there were missiles in the world that weren't being accounted for, and where in the world were they? Khrushchev only fed this, baiting the world that of course they had more missiles than anyone suspected they did, that they "turned them out like sausages," and that they could be anywhere in the world. Naturally, after the Bay of Pigs invasion, Cuba's success, and the Soviet celebration of that success, the U.S. could only conclude some of those missiles were indeed in Cuba, with crazy Castro's finger on the button.

There was that, and there was also information that was leaked to the States about everything and anything going on in Cuba, that Khrushchev had armed Cuba to help them protect themselves from another U.S. invasion. "Those who were disaffected by the Revolution would send messages any way they could to the United States, informing their family members and the [government] functionaries of the movements they were observing. The press wasn't long in echoing the rumors."

So Cuba had nukes, they were mad at the capitalist world, and they had Soviet support for whatever they wanted to do. It created a precarious situation for the U.S. and the world at large. Castro asked for Khrushchev's support and he had it. Though Castro said, "I added that it would be inconsistent of us to expect the maximum support from the USSR and the rest of the socialist camp should be attacked by the United States and yet refuse to face the political risks and the possible damages to our reputation when they needed us. The ethical and revolutionary point of view was accepted unanimously."

The crisis, sparked by this knowledge, would last 13 days in October 1962. It was essentially a standoff, and the world feared the outcome. The USSR would be shipping more nukes to Cuba, and the U.S. planned to block the shipment from coming through. Cuba and the Soviet Union would not accept what they perceived as "outright piracy," and promised to retaliate. Castro said, "This was no longer a question that had to do with tactics or strategy. It was a decision that had to do with the willingness, or lack thereof, to maintain a firm stance in the situation that had emerged."

As the tension mounted, what had been a three-headed monster was reduced to two when Kennedy reached out to Khrushchev, without Castro, to make an arrangement, despite the fact that Khrushchev had already assured the U.S. in a letter that there would be no way the USSR was going to back down from what he called "an act of aggression propelling humankind into the abyss of a world nuclear-missile war." Namely, the aggression of the U.S. to blockade a vessel from the Soviet Union to Cuba, no matter what the contents of that vessel might be. It was a violation for the U.S. to interfere with "navigation in international waters and air space," and it would not be tolerated. Castro never believed Khrushchev would bend. He recalled: ". . . it was a very tense moment. And we ourselves thought that conflict was inevitable . . . It never occurred to us to give in to the adversary's threats."

But it had occurred to Khrushchev, and, Castro felt, behind his back. On October 23, Soviet ships headed towards the blockade as the world sat back, helpless to prevent the inevitable nuclear war about to occur.

Finally, on October 28, 1962, Khrushchev reached an agreement with Kennedy whereby he would destroy USSR missiles in Cuba if Kennedy agreed to dismantle U.S. missiles in Turkey and Italy. And that was it. The Soviet ships turned around and the crisis was averted. But not without bitterness on Castro's part. He felt betrayed by Khrushchev; left out and belittled. While the two would see their way back to the camaraderie they had enjoyed, the initial blow of what Castro saw as a betrayal would burn for quite some time.

CHAPTER TWENTY-FOUR
CASTRO AND KENNEDY

"[Kennedy] spoke on television 22 October, at 7 p.m. His speech was carried by every network, with a great sense of drama, and at that point the world became aware that there was this crisis and that we were on the brink of a nuclear war. And he also announced a naval blockade of Cuba, in order to prevent the arrival of more missiles."

The relationship between Fidel Castro and American President John Fitzgerald Kennedy is not an easy one to define; namely because there was no "relationship" between them. In the two conflicts that are pretty much the most significant of the rulership of both leaders, one who would lead more than four decades and one who would lead less than four years, there wasn't direct contact between them. Castro negotiated with the CIA on the terms for releasing prisoners after the Bay of Pigs invasion; and Castro was left out of the negotiations between Kennedy and Khrushchev following the Cuban Missile Crisis. Though it had come out later that both men were open to discussions, it just never happened. Perhaps had Kennedy lived, things would have been different between

Cuba and the U.S. today. Perhaps some middle ground could have been reached, communication opened, embargoes lifted. But that was not to be.

One really couldn't draw the assumption that the Bay of Pigs invasion would not have happened had Kennedy been at the helm while the Cuban Revolution was happening, but Castro managed to do just that. He respected Kennedy, and truly believed that Kennedy would have been more rational and balanced when it came to the situation in Cuba, and how it might have impacted the United States. Castro cited that Kennedy, even giving the official go-head on the attack on the Bay of Pigs, was the one who ended it. "[A]t that moment, Kennedy showed himself to be reasonable—he refused to complicate things; he gave the order to suspend the 'reconnaissance' flights, the low-level espionage flights, and also ordered that Operation Mongoose be halted."

Yet Kennedy and his influence cannot be discounted in the shaping of Fidel's experience as a leader. Despite that the two major incidents involving the United States, the two major threats on Cuba, had transpired during Kennedy's rule, Castro had an enormous amount of respect for John Fitzgerald Kennedy, in the face of anything he was handed. Castro said, "... President John Kennedy, a guy with a great deal of talent, really, had the misfortune to inherit the expedition against us, the Playa Girón invasion—he inherited it and he let it take place. He was brave in defeat; because he assumed all responsibility for it, he put it this way: 'Victory has a thousand fathers, but defeat is an orphan.'"

That same elegance that earned Castro's respect, however, also made him know that with those words, Kennedy would be berated or worse by his own people, the American capitalists who opposed Castro and everything he stood for. Castro said, "All of that created an intense hatred of Kennedy on the part of all the adversaries of the Cuban Revolution, because he didn't give the order for the fleet to step in during Playa Girón to help the mercenaries, and he didn't take advantage of the October crisis to intervene against us as many generals and many of our enemies were advising him to. That may be who was behind the conspiracy to assassinate him. Although I have no proof, I am making deductions about what may have happened. I daresay that it's true though—there are many, many reasons to be suspicious."

Interesting that Fidel could see that Kennedy would make enemies who would want him removed, even as some have suggested that Castro himself not only knew that the assassination would occur, but that he might even have had a hand in it, even as an accomplice. It has been suggested that Lee Harvey Oswald came to Cuba and got assistance from Castro to carry out Kennedy's murder. As Castro clearly understood that Kennedy was not behind the conflicts between the U.S. and Cuba, and that Kennedy probably would not have acted in the way he did had the cart not already been in motion, it does seem far-fetched that someone who might come to have some sympathy and understanding for Cuba would have something to do with his removal.

Castro doesn't give those conspiracies much weight. In fact, Oswald had attempted to come to Cuba, and he was refused. Castro said, "Thank goodness we didn't give that guy permission to visit Cuba. That would have been a tremendous manipulation, a tremendous provocation, because provocation—because they could have used that to implicate Cuba. Actually, when the investigation was being carried out, we gave them all the information we had."

Of course, just because Castro didn't let Oswald into the country before the assassination didn't prove he had any knowledge of the plan to take down Kennedy, nor does Castro believe that Oswald was the only assassin. Castro said, "With the expertise I had acquired in sharpshooting, I can't imagine that with a rifle with a telescopic sight such as he had, you can fire, load, and fire gain in a matter of seconds. Because when you shoot with a telescopic sight, if the weapon moves a fraction of an inch, you lose your target." He added, "Firing three times in a row, so accurately, somebody who almost certainly didn't have much experience—that's very difficult."

During Kennedy's term, Castro's opinion of him never wavered, even when he experienced Kennedy trying to enforce, unsuccessfully, some of Castro's planned reforms throughout Latin America, including widespread agrarian reform. Kennedy may have been trying to do what he thought was right, but it didn't work. Castro said, ". . . many Latin American rulers stole all the money they could and the Alliance for Progress didn't solve a thing. Still, it was an intelligent reaction on Kennedy's part—he was a man of unquestionable intelligence."

CHAPTER TWENTY-FIVE

REACHING OUT TO LATIN AMERICA AND BEYOND

"Current and future generations of Cubans will continue on, no matter how great the difficulties may be, fighting tirelessly to ensure that the Revolution is always as invulnerable politically as it is militarily and will soon be economically. We will continue to fight. We will continue to resist. We will continue to defeat every imperialist aggression, every lie in their propaganda, every political and diplomatic maneuver."

While Castro's main concern had always been the health and well-being of his beloved Cuba, as a true revolutionary he knew it was important to try to help the greater good, to improve the world, by spreading the healing fundamentals of his revolutionary ideas beyond Cuba, and enriching Latin America as a whole while he was at it. He said, "More than 820 million people in the world suffer from hunger, and 790 million of them live in the Third World."

As Castro explained, "Back at that time, in the '60s, no

one in Latin America maintained diplomatic relations with us—Mexico was the only one. At that time, we observed all international rules of conduct. We did, of course, want revolution; we desired it out of doctrine, out of conviction. But we observed international law. And I maintain that revolution can't be exported, because no one can 'export' the objective conditions that make revolution possible. That has always been our premise and we still think that way."

Castro contends that his main objective was to help, not to take over, though his actions were not always perceived in the way he intended they be perceived. For example, when he went to Buenos Aries in the early 1960s, the homeland of his comrade, Che Guevara, to discuss how best to take advantage of the Alliance for Progress in Latin America, he didn't quite meet his objectives. "I didn't have much international experience, except all the things I'd read throughout my life and of course my own meditations on the subject. Nor did I have much experience with Latin America, but I presented this plan there anyway."

His ideas did not go over as planned and he backed down. Then President Kennedy came back with another way to present the plan. Castro said of his own agenda, "The plan would've helped avoid many tragedies on this continent." He contends that it would have been the best-case scenario, even as a short time later, "Kennedy picked up the idea and poised his own Marshall Plan for Latin America—the Alliance for Progress: agrarian reform, fiscal reform, housing and construction . . ." That, as history shows, was also not a success, with many countries stealing and misappropriating funds.

But Fidel was undeterred. Just because all the facts pointed to this being a time ripe for change in Latin America didn't mean the people were ready or willing to embrace revolution, and Fidel accepted that, to a point. As he explains, "Sometimes objective conditions exist for revolutionary change but the subjective conditions aren't there. It was the factors of a subjective nature that prevented the revolution, at that time, from really spreading the method of armed struggle was proven."

That didn't mean Castro turned his back on those who didn't readily jump on the revolution train. Not even in a small way. Fidel remained stalwart in helping the unfortunate, and readily gave aid even when it wasn't being asked. Castro said, "I should say we contributed a great deal to the unity of those people in Nicaragua, in El Salvador, in Guatemala. To the Sandinistas, who were divided; the Salvadorians, who were divided into something like five organizations; the Guatemalans, who were equally fragmented. Our mission, as we saw it, was to unite, and we managed to unite, really. We have shown our solidarity, and we have give some modest aid to the revolutionaries of Central America. But showing solidarity and giving some form of aid to a revolutionary movement doesn't mean you've exported revolution."

In this frenzy of wanting to change the world one nation at a time, Fidel Castro kept a cool, calculating head; not so the case for Che Guevara, however. Che was anxious—almost too anxious—to revolutionize Bolivia, and his fervent intent was starting to make Castro nervous. "We suggested that he needed more time, not to get impatient," Castro said. But Che was insistent, and Castro understood why. He recalled, "He knew what life as a guerrilla was like; he knew you needed to be a certain age, and although he overcame all his own shortcomings and had a will of iron, he knew that if he waited much longer, he wouldn't be in the best physical condition."

Castro knew that this was not the time to start monkeying around in Bolivia, however. There was more organizing that needed to be done, more groundwork to be laid. So he tried to distract Che from Bolivia with another still incredibly worthy cause: He sent him to the Congo.

The Congo Crisis began in 1960 and ran until 1966. The Congo was desperate to gain independence from Belgium and when all was said and done, more than 100,000 would be killed, including Prime Minster Patrice Lumumba. This was a crisis after the Revolutionaries' own hearts, and a perfect place for Che to be while more preparations were being made for Bolivia. Castro said, "When Che got impatient and wanted to leave, I said to him, 'The conditions aren't ready.' I didn't want him to go to Bolivia to organize a tiny group. I wanted him to wait until a larger force had been organized."

So off to the Congo Che went. It would not be the last time Cuba came to the aid of Africa, but this mission was important. Che arrived in the Congo in April 1965 and led the Cuban operation there. The operation was a disaster, which Che would later attribute to the Congolese army. Most of his men were killed, and he returned to Cuba with six other survivors barely six months later.

Castro said, "[Che] ran up against very great obstacles in Africa . . . At a certain point all kinds of people, mercenaries started cropping up: whites, South Africans, Rhodesians, Belgians, and even counter-revolutionary Cubans who were working for the CIA. The African forces weren't prepared. Che wanted to teach them how to fight, explain that there were [sic] sometimes more than one way to do something, that there were variants."

Now Castro had an impatient Che to contend with, and a situation in Bolivia that wasn't ready for him. It didn't matter; Castro could not stop him. What would stop Che, however, was that he and his men were grossly unprepared to take on the cause there, and Che did not have his asthma medication, which meant he would not be in his top form on top of everything else.

On October 8, 1967, Che and his men were captured. Castro said, "Che wasn't a man to allow himself to be captured, but a bullet had ruined his rifle, and the enemy soldiers, very close by now, wounded him. He was wounded and weaponless, and that's why they captured him . . . The next day, 9 October 1967, at noon, he was cold-bloodedly executed. I'm certain he never flinched, never trembled once, because when he was faced with a situation of dangers was when he stood tallest."

Even without his beloved comrade at his side, however, Castro remained faithful to the cause of Revolution. Over the next decades, he and his brother Raul would keep Cuba under control, despite the most of the world being against them.

CHAPTER TWENTY-SIX

CASTRO AND THE FALL OF THE USSR

"History will pronounce the final judgment on him. I do not want to be Gorbachev's judge. I can only say that during the time I knew him, he behaved in a friendly manner toward me. He seemed to want to improve socialism, even if the final result was different. He wrote it in his book Perestroika too, making it clear that he was not against socialism, indeed he wanted more socialism. It seems to me, however, that now there is less socialism than ever in the former USSR—and indeed the USSR does not even exist anymore. Someone once said that the road to hell is paved with good intentions."

For decade of his reign, Fidel and Cuba were intensely dependent on the USSR for survival—for protection and economics. The agreements made between Khrushchev and Castro during Castro's 1963 visit to the Soviet Union stood the test of time. Throughout the 1970s and 1980s, the relationship was strong, even with Gorbachev at the helm, at least for a while. Castro said, "There were good relations with [Mikhail] Gorbachev. Raul had known him for years . . . I talked to him quite a bit, I met him, conversed with him often . . . With us he was very friendly, he behaved like a friend, really, and one could see his respect for the Cuban Revolution."

It seemed the Soviet Union would always be there for Cuba. Castro never imagined in a million years that the Soviet Union could implode the way it had. But that was the reality of the legacy Gorbachev had somehow managed to create, and then abandon with his resignation the day before the dissolution became formal on December 26, 1991.

A little background: The Soviet economy had been stagnant since the 1980s, and Gorbachev had tried to revive it by increasing liberalization, but his plan backfired. Without the one-party structure that had sustained the nation, disputes began to spark, nationalist movements among the republics caused discord, and various revolutions led to more democracy, which the USSR could not sustain. Castro said, "I can't say that Gorbachev played a conscious part in the destruction of the Soviet Union, because I have no doubt that Gorbachev's aim was to struggle to perfect socialism." Except that wasn't how things turned out.

Now, as 1992 loomed, Cuba was looking at a chaos where they once had a stabilizer; here was a communist empire that was now shattered to bits.Castro said, "When the Soviet Union and the socialist camp disappeared, no one could have wagered one cent on the survival of the Cuban Revolution."

Those who bet against them would be wrong, but it would take some doing to get Cuba back on strong legs. While the Eastern Bloc's Council for Mutual Economic Assistance provided Cuba 63 percent of its imported food, 86 percent of imported primary goods, and 75 percent of manufactured goods, and purchased 63 percent of Cuba's exported sugar, 72 percent of nickel exports, and 95 percent of its tropical fruit, as well as purchased sugar at prices substantially higher than the world market prices, the fall of the USSR should have meant the fall of Cuba. But no. Cuba knew it had to open to trade with other nations, and made concessions to do so. In doing so, while there may have been some hardship and adversity involved, they managed to hold on.

Still, it was a blow to Cuba, having the superpower they depended on dissipate and disintegrate as it did, and it was hard not to put the blame somewhere. Castro explained, "I'm not interested in defending any of the bad things that the Soviets did. I should make that clear. I came to think, and I still think this way today, that without the accelerated industrialization that country was forced to engage in, largely because of the west, which blockaded them, invaded them, and made war on them, the USSR would never have been saved by Nazi onslaught; they'd have been defeated. In the middle of the war, they were able to transport factories and set them down right there in the snow and start production without even a roof over them—it was a great feat, maybe one of the greatest feats in that war in which so many previous political mistakes had been made, that is where I would be most critical of the errors they made."

Still, it was shocking that a nation that had always proven so resourceful could not get out of their own way when it came to growing their economy. As Castro related, "What's curious is that the USSR had more research centers than any other country, carried out more research projects, and, except in the military spheres, applied fewer of its own findings to the benefits of its own economy."

If anything, the fall of the USSR was an educational experience. Not only did it force Cuba to reach out to the rest of the world and expand their relationships, but it forced them to look within to how they were advancing, especially when it came to computer technology in Cuba. Castro said, "[I]t's a lack of vision. It's shocking, sobering, while the Yankees, on the other hand, developed computers as fast as they could."

Did Castro ultimately blame Gorbachev for the fall of the USSR? He almost had to. "[A]t one point of his leadership I had a terrible opinion of everything Gorbachev was doing," Castro said, despiteliking Gorbachev and thinking he was trying. "But he couldn't manage to find solutions to the big problems his country had . . . He couldn't prevent the disintegration of the Soviet Union; he didn't know how to preserve it, keep it a great nation and a great power. On the contrary, his errors and later weaknesses contributed to [the collapse]."

CHAPTER TWENTY-EIGHT

EMIGRATION ISSUES

"In 1958, the official number of Cubans officially registered in the United States stood at about 125,000, including descendants [of immigrants]. That was before 1959, not long after the end of the war, fascism, the Holocaust, all of those things. Each year, they would issue 2,000 or 3,000 visas, if that many. Power, wealth—many people brought up to worship in the United States, and above all, to idealize (remember this, it's important) the automobile, resources, salaries, in a Cuban population who had little or no education and in which over 30 percent were either illiterate or semiliterate."

The emigration situation has long been a source of confusion, aggravation, and resentment between Cuba and the rest of the world. It is interesting to note, however, that the situation is not all the doing of Fidel Castro. In fact, there's a long history of emigration issues, beginning with the situation that arose of people shipping their kids into the United States during Operation Peter Pan.

As a result of all those unaccompanied minors popping up in Miami in the early 1960s, in October 1962, the U.S.

halted all flights between Cuba and the U.S. The emigration was out of control and could not be monitored. "So," Castro said, "there was no longer any possibility of travel, and many families became separated. Many of the parents who'd sent their children up there were still thinking that the Revolution was going to fail, and some of them were separated forever."

It wasn't just the kids that were creating an issue, though. There was an exodus of all ages from Cuba at overthrowing of the Batista regime. Scores of middle- and upper-class people flocked to the United States to, as they believed, wait out the unrest. They believed the U.S., or somebody, would unseat the new rebel-ruled regime. It never happened, and the Cuban population exploded in Miami, with emigres thinking they'd only stay months now looking to stay forever. So illegal departures from Cuba, those that were not explained to and authorized by the government, were halted.

But that couldn't last forever; there had to be some kind of agreement put in place for Cubans to leave the country, to travel to the United States, or anywhere, for that matter. "So then an agreement was reached with the United States," Castro explained. "Every person who applied, who had some notion of going to the United States, could do so legally. We ourselves obtained that permission."

Things quieted for a while; then came the Carioca exodus. The early 1960s were a time of struggle while the Revolution settled in. There was fallout from the Bay of Pigs invasion, the Missile Crisis; specialists were leaving the country, trade was stifled, food and other stuff were being rationed. People lost faith that any of this was ever going to work out. Castro said, "The Carioca exodus happened in October 1965. And shortly afterwards, in November 1966, the Americans—I honestly don't know why—passed the Adjustment Act."

The Adjustment Act, or, formally, the Cuban Refugee Adjustment Act, which was passed on November 2, 1966, and signed into law by President Lyndon Johnson, essentially made anyone who came into the United States by legal means, and had resided in the States for at least a year, permanent resident status.

There wouldn't be another significant emigration crisis again until the 1980s, when Ronald Reagan was in office.

In 1980, there was another mass exodus from Cuba, this one also spurned by a sharp economic turndown in the Cuban economy. The "Mariel Crisis" was named for the Mariel boatlift, a mass emigration of Cubans that left Cuba via Mariel Harbor between April and October of 1980. The Cuban government allowed anyone who wanted to leave to do so, and the American government granted them entry, though there was backlash when it was discovered that most of the refugees who had entered had come from prisons or mental institutions. Both governments agreed to shut it down, though not before 125,000 Cubans had come to Florida.

In 1984, the Reagan Administration granted passage again between Florida and Cuba. Castro said, "He was flexible in that, because of his interest in returning the 'excludables.' Reagan was interested in an agreement on the so-called 'excludables,' some of the people who'd left in the Mariel exodus in 1980 and the United States wanted to return to us ... The American authorities would issue up to 20,000 visas a year [under the agreement], which would ensure that the number of people wouldn't have to put their lives in danger to make the trip."

Sounded like a good agreement, except that, Castro complained, the Americans did not hold up their end of the bargain. Castro said, ". . . the most visas they ever issues totaled no more than a thousand and something . . ." So much for Castro thinking relations could improve between the United States and Cuba. In fact, seen though Castro's eyes, the situation would only get worse.

Following the fall of the USSR in 1991, there was another, expected, economic downturn, until Cuba could get in place the other trade agreements it knew it had to establish to survive. Rationing became *de rigueur* once again, and once again, Cubans fled. Castro said, "The exodus of 1994 was brought on by the Soviet crisis, the fall of the USSR, the beginning of the special period in Cuba. And during that time, the United States was issuing fewer than 1,000 visas a year . . ." With President Bill Clinton leading the nation, Castro said, "In 1994, fewer than 1,000 people were allowed to leave the island legally with visas, and then about 5,000 or 6,000 left illegally, in order to take advantage of the Adjustment Act—despite Reagan's promise to issue up to 20,000 visas a year."

People thought they could go to the United States, stay a year, and always be able to stay. The trouble was, they needed those visas to stay that year, and they weren't getting them. Castro said, "The Adjustment Act has caused the loss of no one knows how many lives—thousands of lives. They never even report all the names of the people who reach [the United States], whether anyone died [in the crossing]—never! Cuba is the only country in the world that brutal law is applied to!"

Castro has his own system in place for people leaving Cuba. He said, "For over 40 years, every person who leaves

Cuba is an 'exile,' an 'enemy of the socialist regime.'" Once you were gone, for Castro, it seemed you were dead; except then why make exceptions? It was a very confusing situation, but the issues and the animosity were not Castro's alone. He explained, "For coming to Cuba or for any other violation of the blockade, an American citizen can be sent to prison. And if I'm not mistaken, there's a fine of up to $250,000 for visiting Cuba without permission. The fine can be as much as a million dollars in the case of a corporation."

This was the case in the early 2000s; there had been another exodus, mainly of young people, under Raul Castro's reign. In June 2010, U.S. and Cuban officials sat down to discuss the issue more closely, but the situation would not be quickly resolved.

CHAPTER TWENTY-FIVE

CASTRO IN AFRICA

"I should tell you that while Cuba was in Angola and Angola was being invaded by South Africa, the United States made arrangements to transfer to South Africa racist, fascist South Africa—several atomic bombs, similar to those it exploded in Hiroshima and Nagasaki, which means that this war in Angola—this is something that people often forget—was fought by Cuban and Angolan soldiers against an army and a government that had right atom bombs, provided by the United States through that great supporter, that eternal supported of the blockade, Israel . . . [W]e took all precautions . . . that the South Africans were going to drop a nuclear weapon on our troops."

Che had been sent to the Congo in the mid 1960s, both to distract him from his fixation on Bolivia, and also to help the Congolese people fight for their independence from Belgian rule; overthrowing imperialism being a cause close to the Revolution's heart. The situation in the Congo had been a mess, however, and Che returned after only several months of fighting. Later, he would address the UN. As Castro recalled, "In [Che Guevara's] speech to the UN General Assembly on 11 December 1964, he had strongly denounced the American and Belgian aggression against the Congo. He said something like this—I am quoting from memory, 'Every free man in the world must be ready to avenge the crime committed against the Congo.'"

Che's foray into the Congo wasn't the first and wasn't Cuba's final foray into Africa, however. Recalled Castro, "In 1961—not two years after [our] victory, when the people of Algeria were still fighting for their independence—a Cuban ship took weapons to the Algerian patriots. And on its return to Cuba, brought back about 100 children who had been orphaned and wounded in the war."

It wasn't only soldiers who were sent to Algeria. Castro said, "Several Cuban doctors were sent to Algeria to help the people there. And that was the way we started, 44 years ago, what is today and extraordinary medical collaboration with the nations of the third world."

After the intervention in the Congo, the Cubans would return, this time to deal with the bleak situation in South Africa. One of the most significant conflicts in Africa that Fidel got Cuba involved in was the Angola Civil War. In November 1975, Cuba joined the leftist People's Movement for the Liberation of Angola (MPLA), and by the end of 1975, the number of troops in Angola was more than 25,000. Castro said, "If you're weak with security, you're defeated. You have to be willing to send in all the forces needed, then an additional number of forces, twice or even three times the original number."

Castro was fully committed to the situation in Angola, and his devotion would win him a lifetime friendship with Nelson Mandela, himself a revolutionary who had been imprisoned for fighting for his beliefs, who ultimately came to power. Said Castro of his and Cuba's involvement in Angola, "Our collaboration with the independence struggle in Angola and Guinea-Bissau began in 1965, and it consisted essentially of preparing fighting units and sending in instructors and material aid."

After one of the bloodier battles in Angola, Cuba opened its arms and its borders to children who had been affected in the Cassinga Massacre. As Castro recalled, "It was one of those actions on that war with the most causalities, counting both dead and wounded. But the massacre was stopped, and the hundreds of surviving or wounded children were brought to Cuba to recover. They were later enrolled in school, where they received their primary and middle school education. Some of them later graduated from Cuban universities," he said. In fact, he said, "In 1978, . . . the survivors of the Cassinga Massacre arrived, the great majority of whom were children."

Castro's devotion to helping out in Africa seems to stem from his ever-abiding sense of injustice and wanting basic human rights for all, though tinged with wanting to go against what the Americans and Europeans were doing. Castro said, " . . . I don't think Cuba's heroic solidarity with our sister nations in Africa has been well enough recognized. That glorious page of our revolutionary history deserves to be known, even if only to encourage the hundreds of thousands of men and women who are internationalist combatants . . . Nor, in my opinion, are people sufficiently knowledgeable about the history of Europe's imperialist and neo-colonial looting and pillaging of Africa, with, of course, the full support of the United States and NATO."

CHAPTER TWENTY-NINE
CUBAN ECONOMICS

"The country resisted, and it made considerable progress on the social front. Today, it has recovered more of its nutritional requirements and is making rapid progress on other fronts. And even under those conditions, the work done and the awareness created for years produced a miracle. Why did we resist? Because the Revolution had, has, and increasingly will have the support of a nation, an intelligent populace which is increasingly untied, educated, and combative."

Since the Revolution, Cuba has struggled with economic downturns on several occasions, though not necessarily more than other countries may have. Some of these downturns are directly related to policies, and politics; others have to do with the state of the world.

First, some background on Cuban economics since the country won its independence. The Cuban War for Independence in the 1890s marked one of the first economic downturns, as Cuba struggled to break free from Spain and the sugar plantation, many American-owned at the time, suffered—and with it, the Cuban economy.

During World War I, the demand for sugar rose, and Cuba became a major supplier and enjoyed a prosperous number of years, but the economy tanked again after the war when the demand leveled off. The sharp economic downturn suffered by the rest of the world as a result of the war didn't help matters any, as Cuban sugar farmers, now in deep debt, lost their farms to foreclosure. The banks also found themselves in dire straits.

By the late 1920s, the economy was back on an upswing, but not for everyone. Student groups, including *Federación Estudiantil Universitaria* (FEU) (the Federation of University Students), a group that Castro himself would become involved in, were formed, as was a desire on behalf of those not succeeding to do something about corruption in the government under President Gerardo Machado. Labor unions were started and the Communist Party of Cuba was formed in 1925 as a result of workers seeking revolution.

A situation of political unrest and a labor strike in 1933 led to U.S. intervention, via an ambassador sent from FDR. Machado was overthrown, Batista took control of the army, and Ramon Grau become the new head of the government, though his leadership would be short-lived because it wasn't recognized by the U.S. government. Batista appointed Carlos Mendieta, who was recognized, and the economy stabilized.

Then Batista came to power for the first time. Under Batista, the economy was good. During this presidency, he promoted social welfare and even had the support of the Communist Party. After his run, however, he went into exile in the U.S., first depleting the treasury and making it difficult for the newly elected president, Ramon Grau again, to govern.

This period, the early 1940s, is significant here as Castro was in school at the time, forming his ideas about the world and how things should be running, especially when it came to Cuba. The Grau government was corrupt, and essentially took money from the people. He was "replaced" via military coup, with Batista taking over and the economy thriving for those in power, and squashing others. This was where Castro came in.

The first years of the Revolution were not easy economically as social reform and nationalization were being ironed out, but soon the economy was back on its feet. Castro made friends with the USSR in the 1960s, and despite cutting off trade with the U.S. and others, and with some dips here and there, kept the Cuban economy stable over the years. When sugar prices dropped, the economy grew with tourism and through other means throughout the 1970s and 1980s.

It wasn't until the fall of the USSR that Cuba hit a deep recession, which began even before the Soviet Union collapsed. The Soviet economy itself had been struggling financially for years before the collapse, but the dissolution hit Cuba hard, economically speaking. Castro said, "The country took a stunning blow when, from one day to the next, that great power collapsed and left us out in the cold, all by ourselves, and we lost all our markets for sugar, we stooped receiving foodstuffs, fuel, even the wood to bury our dead in. From one day to the next, we found ourselves without fuel, without raw materials, without food, without soap, without everything."

In the years that followed, Fidel struggled to make new alliances and improve the Cuban economy. Castro explained, "Our basic problems are the economic blockade and the disappearance of the socialist camp. Some 85 percent of our trade was with those countries and we had reasonable prices—let us say the right prices. The value of our sugar, in fact, balanced the cost of the petroleum we got from the USSR. Our exports reached 80 billion [currency not stated] or just under. That trade has almost disappeared with the disappearance of the socialist countries. We have had to turn to new markets. We have lost imports, credit, and technology, and sought fuel, raw materials, and drugs elsewhere. Our sugar is no longer quoted at that price . . . To this must be added the fact that we are under a severe economic blockade from the United States."

In addition to making new alliances and trade partners, including a healthy relationship with Venezuela that lasted years, the Cuban economy has recovered due to better economic planning and limited private enterprise. While sugar is still the main crop grown and exported, a percentage of the land has been reallocated to other crops.

The Cuban economy, while not alone in the world in this, is now struggling. To this end, the new leader, Raul Castro is working to initiate reforms to stimulate the economy. When asked by *Atlantic Monthly* reporter Jeffrey Goldberg if "Cuba's model—Soviet-style communism—was still worth exporting to other countries," Castro replied, "The Cuban model doesn't even work for us anymore." It will be interesting to see in the coming decades what will work.

CHAPTER THIRTY

CASTRO AND NELSON MANDELA

"Long live the Cuban Revolution. Long live comrade Fidel Castro . . . Cuban internationalists have done so much for African independence, freedom, and justice. We admire the sacrifices of the Cuban people in maintaining their independence and sovereignty in the face of a vicious imperialist campaign designed to destroy the advances of the Cuban revolution. We too want to control our destiny . . . There can be no surrender. It is a case of freedom or death. The Cuban revolution has been a source of inspiration to all freedom-loving people."
—*Nelson Mandela*

To understand Nelson Mandela's passion for Castro, for his work and his ideals, it's important to appreciate where Nelson Mandela is coming from. A little background on Mandela: As a South African political activist who waged for decades against apartheid, Mandela became the first elected president of South Africa in 1994, and the first black man to hold the office. Mandela was elected just four years after serving a 27-year-long prison sentence after being arrested as one of eight men accused of conspiracy to overthrow the government and sabotage in the Rivonia Trial, and was sentenced to life in prison.

Said Mandela before his conviction, "During my lifetime I have dedicated myself to this struggle of the African people. I have fought against white domination, and I have fought against black domination. I have cherished the ideal of a democratic and free society in which all persons live together in harmony and with equal opportunities. It is an ideal for which I hope to live, and to see realized. But my Lord, if it needs be, it is an ideal for which I am prepared to die."

Mandela, like Castro, was born into a family of means—royalty, actually—and was given every opportunity possible. And Mandela, like Castro, became deeply involved in overturning oppression on underprivileged people as a young man at school. Like Castro, he studied to become a lawyer, and unlike Castro, became committed to nonviolent protest. Along with the South African Communist Party, Mandela cofounded the uMkhonto we Sizwe (MK, "Spear of the Nation"), the armed wing of the African National Congress.

Interestingly enough, while Mandela was older than Castro, he has said that the Cuban Revolution strongly influenced his own political convictions and actions, and that Castro's troops in Angola during the 1970s and 1980s were instrumental in overturning apartheid and legitimizing the African National Congress.

The feeling was mutual, however. Castro said, ". . . Nelson Mandela is one of the men I admire most, because of his merits and his history, his struggle." The feeling between the two men was mutual. While Mandela was in prison while Castro sent troops to fight against apartheid in Angola in the 1970s, he was well aware of the fight the Cuban leader was waging against the racism both men abhorred.

Castro sent more than 300,000 Cuban troops to South Africa to support independence, and was an instrumental figure in the fight Nelson Mandela spent his life, and would have given his life, to fight. His efforts on behalf of South Africa did not go unrecognized by Mandela.

One of the first trips Mandela made upon his release from prison in 1990 was to visit Fidel Castro in Cuba for three days, where he celebrated the man who had helped out his country so much. For this, however, he was highly criticized by the American government. In Florida, five Cuban-American mayors signed a declaration demanding Mandela renounce Castro, and controversy persisted around his devotion to Fidel. He praised Castro, "Who trained our people, who gave us resources, who helped so many of our soldiers, our doctors?"

Fidel Castro returned the admiration, stating, "If you want an example of a firm, valiant, heroic, serene, intelligent and capable man, this example, this man, is Mandela."

Interestingly enough, Fidel Castro hadn't been to South Africa during the whole time his troops fought there. When Mandela asked him when he was coming, Castro responded, "I have not visited my homeland South Africa, but I love it as if it were my homeland."

In 1994, Castro would make the trip, however. When Mandela was elected president of South Africa, Fidel Castro was the guest of honor. Said Mandela of Castro, "What Fidel [Castro] has done for us is difficult to describe with words. First in the struggle against apartheid he did not hesitate to give us all his help and now that we are free, we have many Cuban doctors working here [in South Africa]."

At one point, Castro brought up the war in Angola with Mandela, curious to know where some weapons ended up. Castro said, "One day I asked Nelson Mandela, 'Mr. President, do you know where the weapons that South Africa had are?' 'No, I don't know.' 'What have the South African military leaders told you?' 'They haven't told me a word.' That's a time that nobody knows about, and the world doesn't ask those questions, ever, anyone."

While the friendship between Castro and Mandela was strong and long-lived, formal diplomatic relations between the two countries did not exist before 1994. The relationship Mandela had with Fidel and Cuba allowed him to open doors of communication with other Latin American countries, including Argentina, Brazil, Peru, and Chile.

As important as Castro was in South Africa, so was Mandela in Cuba. Cuba even celebrates Nelson Mandela International Day every July 18th.

On Mandela's 90th birthday, Castro wrote, in celebration of the great leader, "Glory to you, Nelson, who while in prison for 25 years defended human dignity! Slander and hatred could do nothing against your endurance of steel. You were able to resist and, without knowing or looking for it, you became a symbol of what is most noble in humanity. You will live in the memory of future generations, and in your memory the Cubans who died defending the liberty of their brothers in other lands of the world."

Mandela died on December 5, 2013.

CHAPTER THIRTY-ONE
CASTRO AND CHÁVEZ

"Without a man like Hugo Chávez, who was born in humble circumstances and educated under the disciplined eyes of military academies in Venezuela, where so many ideas of Latin American freedom, unity, and integration were taught by [Simon] Bolivar, there would never have emerged at this decisive moment in our hemisphere a process of such historical and international transcendence as the revolutionary process in this country."

Fidel Castro was 28 years older than Hugo Chávez, but Chávez was an incredibly important figure in Fidel's life, and in the life of the Cuban nation in general, following the 1991 crumbling of the USSR and the economic turmoil that wrought in Cuba. While he wouldn't come to power until he was voted into office during the 1998 election in Venezuela, Chávez had been making a name for himself since the early 1990s, and he hadn't gone unnoticed by Castro and company.

Unlike his mentor, Fidel Castro, Chávez came from a working-class background. Born in 1954, he became a career military officer instead of pursuing higher education, and as early as the 1980s, he founded the Revolutionary Bolivarian Movement-200 to overthrow the what he considered the corrupt Venezuelan political system. He was imprisoned following an unsuccessful coup he led against President Carlos Andres Perez in 1992 for two years.

Despite the falling out in the 1960s, Castro had long had his eye on Venezuela as an ally, especially for the oil and wealth of that nation, but it hadn't been possible for him to have his own coup on Romulo Betancourt, who he considered a pawn in the U.S.'s Alliance of Progress "game." That Chávez had tried, even though he failed, was one of the things that endeared Chávez to Castro.

While in prison, Chávez decided he needed to find his way to power, and after his release, he headed to Cuba, because he knew if anyone knew the way to come to power, it was Fidel Castro.

Castro recalled, "Chávez visited us in 1994, nine months after he got out of prison and four years before his first election as president. It was very courageous of him, because he was strongly criticized for coming to Cuba. He came and we talked. We discovered an intelligent man, very progressive, and authentic Bolivarian. Then he won the elections. Several times. He changed the constitution. With formidable support from the people. His adversaries have tried to get rid of him both by force and economics. But he has faced all the oligarchies, all of imperialism's assaults against the Bolivarian process."

In addition to communists Fidel and Raul Castro, Chávez would align himself with heads of socialist governments in Latin America, including Bolivia's Evo Morales, Ecuador's

Rafael Correa, and Nicaragua's Daniel Ortega.

Chávez started a socialist political party called the Fifth Republic Movement and ran for president of Venezuela in 1998; he won, and was again re-elected in 2000; then 2006; then again in 2012.

While his presidency was marked with various socialist successes, including nationalizing key industries, creating worker-managed cooperatives, and introducing Boliviarian Missions and Communal Councils, he also had his share of enemies. Chávez was an outspoken critic of U.S. foreign policy, imperialism, and capitalism; he called George W. Bush a "donkey" and "the devil."

While Venezuela and Cuba had a good relationship in the early 20th century, the Cuban Revolution damaged it. Then in 1961, the then-president of Venezuela, Romulo Betancourt, severed all ties with Cuba, and worked to have Cuba expelled from the Organization of American States in 1964 over controversy involving Cuba taking guerrilla action against Venezuela. Relations were restored, in the 1970s, though they remained strained for various reasons. Chávez would mend those fences, at least at the end of the 20th century and start of the 21st century, while he was president.

Chávez was a huge fan of Castro and his reforms, and praised Castro whenever possible. When he spoke at the University of Havana in 1999, Chávez said, "Venezuela is traveling towards the same sea as the Cuban people, a sea of happiness and of real social justice and peace."

Throughout his presidency, Chávez maintained a close relationship with Castro, which made Venezuelan conservatives incredibly nervous. When in 2000, Chávez signed an agreement that gave Cuba 130,000 subsidized barrels of oil a day on "preferential terms," conservatives got more nervous, even as Cuba sent hundreds of doctors, teachers, and sports trainers to Venezuela in exchange. Chávez said, "Here we are, as alert as ever, Fidel and Hugo, fighting with dignity and courage to defend the interests of our people, and to bring alive the idea of Bolívar and Martí. In the name of Cuba and Venezuela, I appeal for the unity of our two peoples, and of the revolutions that we both lead. Bolívar and Martí, one country united!"

It all worked out great for Cuba, though. The struggle in the decade since the fall of the USSR was alleviated by this "gift." Venezuela wasn't thrilled about it, especially as their economy was shaky at the time. Ramifications would have to follow.

Sure enough, on April 11, 2002, a coup took place to oust Chávez from office. He immediately called Castro for help and advice, as Castro recalled, "We talked about other things: the way he should leave the country temporarily, get in touch with some office with real authority among the coup members, assure them of his willingness to leave the country but not resign. From Cuba . . . we'd try to mobilize the diplomatic corps in our country and Venezuela; we'd send two planes with our foreign minister and a group of diplomats to pick him up. He thought about it for a few seconds, then finally agreed to my idea. It would all depend now on the enemy leader."

The coup had erupted in response to the way it appeared Chávez had been appointing his cronies to top government posts, not qualified people, and the nation was worried this would mean a collapse. Hundreds of thousands of Venezuelans marched against Chávez in Caracas. Following his arrest, thousands more marched the same streets in protest of his arrest. Before he was arrested however, Castro advised him, "'Save those brave men who are with us now in that unnecessary battle.' The idea came from my conviction that if a popular, charismatic leader such as Chávez, toppled in that deceitful way and under those circumstances, wasn't killed, then the people—in this case with the support of the best members of his armed forces—would demand his return, and that return would be inevitable." It had turned out just as Castro had predicted.

During the coup, Castro was doing what he could to help his friend from Cuba. Castro said, "Using a mobile phone and a recorder . . . I'd become a kind of news reporter, receiving and broadcasting news and public statements. I was witness to the formidable counter-coup mounted by the people and the Bolivarian armed forces of Venezuela."

Within a few days, the coup had cooled, and Chávez was back in power. "I had not the slightest doubt that Chávez, in a very short time, would be back, and this time carried on the shoulders of his people and his troops," Castro said. "Now, what I had to do was save him from death."

Chávez was grateful for all Castro had done for him during the crisis, later telling the Cuban Communist Party paper, *Granma*, "Fidel to me is a father, a comrade, a master of perfect strategy."

In 2011, Hugo Chávez was diagnosed with cancer, and he underwent treatment in Cuba where Castro had convinced him, and he believed, he would receive the best care. After a tumor the size of a baseball was removed from his pelvic region, Chávez remained confident that he would recover, and even ran for reelection in 2012—and won. But the cancer returned and proved too aggressive to treat. He died in Venezuela in March 2013.

It was a devastating blow for Fidel. There was the issue that without Chávez in power, Cuba's economy could go south again. Of course, Castro had already handed over the reins of government to Raul. But it was as though Castro had lost his son. "The best friend the Cuban people have had in the course of their history passed away," he wrote after Chávez's death. "Although we knew of his critical state of health, the news was a strong blow."

How relations will go between Cuba and Venezuela remains uncertain. However, what remained was Fidel's loyalty to his fallen comrade. "Not even he suspected how great he was," Castro wrote of Chávez. "Onward to victory always, unforgettable friend!"

CHAPTER THIRTY-TWO

MENDING FENCES

"I seriously hope that Cuba and the United States can eventually respect and negotiate our differences. I believe that there are no areas of contention between us that cannot be discussed and settled within a climate of mutual understanding. But first, of course, it is necessary to discuss our differences. I now believe that this hostility between Cuba and the United States is both unnatural and unnecessary—and it can be eliminated."
—Fidel Castro, from a letter to Lyndon Johnson in the 1960s

Relations between Cuba and the United States weren't just strained since the Bay of Pigs invasion and the Cuban Missile Crisis, or since the Cuban Revolution threatened to bring "the Red Menace" to the west. Cuba had hard feelings with the U.S. even before the Batista's military coup that followed years of him living several years in the United States, building interests he'd serve at the expense of the Cuban people. At least for Cuba, the unease can be traced back to the start of the 20th century, when Cuba was fighting against Spain to gain its independence, and the United States intervened in their own interest. Castro said, "North Americans don't understand . . . that our country is not just Cuba; our country is also humanity." And according to Castro, North Americans would continue not to see.

After Cuba won independence from Spain, the United States, who had helped the cause, finally withdrew troops in 1901, on the condition that Cuba agreed to the Platt Amendment, a document that stipulated that U.S. would be permitted to intervene in Cuban affairs. The Cuban-American Treaty leased Guantanamo Bay to the U.S. This arrangement did not make the Cubans happy, but they went along with it. What choice did they have against a big world power like the U.S.?

But even despite the strain, Cuba and the United States were able to work together. Cuba is a huge exporter of sugar, and until the Revolution in 1959, the United States purchased its sugar from Cuba. Following the Revolution, not only did the U.S. stop buying sugar from Cuba, they also stopped supplying the small island nation with oil. By October 1960, the U.S. had prohibited all trade with Cuba. This was an issue for Cuba, to be sure, but Castro was not going to bend to the whims of capitalism, the system he'd spent his entire life trying to overthrow. "My idea, as the whole world knows, is that the capitalist system now doesn't work either for the United States or the world, driving it from crisis to crisis, which are each time more serious," he said.

While Kennedy didn't side with Cuba when he came to office, he did criticize how things had been handled, explaining, "We let Batista put the U.S. on the side of tyranny, and we did nothing to convince the people of Cuba and Latin America that we wanted to be on the side of freedom." Still, Kennedy went through with the already-planned Bay of Pigs invasion, and throughout his short presidency didn't do anything to try to fix the situation between the U.S. and Cuba. There had been interest on both sides to meet and talk, but nothing ever came of it.

When Lyndon Johnson came to office, there was a little conversation, although despite a small hope of reconciliation, that reconciliation was not going to happen. Later, in the 1970s, a series of hijackings affecting both countries brought them a little closer together, and when Jimmy Carter was elected, he and Castro managed to get along, and even made some headway, relaxing the travel ban somewhat and loosening the embargo. But in the 1980s, when Ronald Reagan came to office, the new president reversed everything Carter had managed to accomplish.

In the 1990s, after first tightening sanctions on American businesses based internationally, President William Jefferson Clinton eased travel restrictions and even allowed two baseball games to be played between Cuba's national team and the Baltimore Orioles in 1999. In 2000, Clinton and Castro actually met and shook hands, and in 2001, the U.S. was permitted to engage in some business in Cuba.

However, when George W. Bush took over, he reversed all the progress and called for even tighter restrictions. When the U.S. was attacked on September 11, 2001, Castro pointed some of the blame at the U.S., but made a measure to mend fences. He also offered aid—money, medicine, doctors. The U.S. flatly refused.

When tragedy struck the U.S. again, when Hurricane Katrina ravaged New Orleans, Castro reached out again. Castro said, "[After Hurricane Katrina], we offered 1,610 doctors, and before a second hurricane came, even more, who'd have been able to save many lives, but the American government's pride dictated that [rather than accept Cuban aid], their own citizens had to die on the roofs of their houses, or on the roofs of hospitals from which no one evacuated them, or in stadiums, or in nursing homes, where some of them were given euthanasia in order to prevent a more horrible death by drowning."

Castro found the situation appalling, and further cemented for him that capitalism is such an evil institution that defending it will allow for unnecessary deaths. He has a similar opinion about the American medical system. Castro said, "In the United States there are millions and millions of immigrants, millions and millions of people who don't have means to pay for medical assistance, while here in Cuba, any citizen has full medical service without anybody every asking how they think, whether they support the blockade, as some miserable mercenaries do. That has never been asked, and never will—ever, of anyone!"

Castro couldn't understand how economics could play such a strong role in the culture of a people, blinding them to anything that makes sense, in his eyes. As he explained, "[the United States] portrays itself as a 'defender of human rights', that's the country that in 1959 tried to leave us without doctors, but was without doctors itself . . ."

In 2009, President Barack Obama once again opened the door of communication between the U.S. and Cuba, but indicated that the embargo would not be lifted unless significant change was made, even, as Castro insists, "Over 90 percent of the members of the United Nations condemn the blockade."

Fidel Castro has spoken in favor of Obama before, saying, upon his election, "The intelligent and noble face of the first black president of the United States since its founding two and one-third centuries ago as an independent republic had transformed itself under the inspiration of Abraham Lincoln and Martin Luther King into a living symbol of the American dream."

However, when Obama quipped that change could be possible and fences could be mended between the U.S. and Cuba if Cuba would bend toward democracy, Castro retaliated, saying, with sarcasm, "How kind! How intelligent! Such kindness still has not allowed him to understand that 50 years of blockade and crimes against our country have not been able to bow our people."

CHAPTER THIRTY-THREE

HEALTH
AND CONSEQUENCES

"Well, I'll tell you, as usual, there's been a lot of speculation about that [fall]. It's true that on 23 June 2001, in El Cotorro, a neighborhood in Havana, on a day of intense heat, and during a speech that lasted more than three hours, broadcast live on television, I had a slight loss of consciousness. Something perfectly excusable. It was a slight fainting spell that lasted no more than a few minutes—due to the heat and the terrible sun. A few hours later, those people up there in Miami were already celebrating . . . It could have happened to anybody that stood that long in such hot sun."

In June of 2001, Fidel Castro was about to turn 75 years old. It was understandable that even a younger man would be affected by midday Caribbean heat, but Fidel foes were quick to excitedly jump on this happening as a harbinger of doom—his doom. Speculation ran rampant that Fidel's health was failing, and some hoped it might be weeks, days even, before Fidel fell for good.

The press was quick to point out every instance that might be a clue that Fidel was on his way out. Take as another example an incident in 2004 when Castro lost his footing and took a tumble, nearly face-planting and ending up with a broken arm. Castro said, "When I came to the area of concrete, about 15 or 20 yards from the first row of seats, I didn't see that the granite pavement was raised. When I stepped out with my left foot, there was no pavement there, my foot found no purchase, and the law of gravity, discovered some time ago by Newton, combined with my forward motion, made me, as I stepped out, lurch forward and fall, in a fraction of a second, onto the pavement . . . It was my own fault. The emotion of that day filled with creations and symbolisms explains my carelessness."

In addition to breaking his arm, he also shattered his kneecap, and neither of those body parts seemed ever to have fully healed.

One of the bigger health issues Fidel faced in later years is a serious bout with acute diverticulitis in 2006. Castro refused a temporary colostomy, and instead insisted the entire procedure take place at once. It didn't take, and Castro's haste, and distaste for wearing a colostomy bag, nearly killed him. Other internal organs became terribly infected, and the doctors had a great deal of trouble getting the situation under control. It was a terrible ordeal. "[T]he only thing I hoped for was for the world to stop," he admitted in an interview for *La Jornada*. "Several times I asked myself if [doctors] were going to let me live in those conditions or if they'd let me die." Within a week, he ended up having to have the colostomy anyway, or else he would have died.

His recovery was slow and painful, and he could not eat solid foods for months, causing him to lose a terrifying amount of weight. "Stretched out on that [hospital] bed, I could only look around me, ignorant about those [medical] devices," he continued. "I didn't know how long that torment would last and the only thing I hoped for was for the world to stop."

Throughout this illness, he stayed out of the public eye. It wasn't until several months later that he'd appeared on camera. Within a few months, he opted to undergo surgery again, to reconnect his intestines. He said, "'I was able to recover full control of my mind, [and] read and meditated a lot.'"

In October 2012, Castro reportedly suffered a "serious embolic stroke" which, doctors said, put him in a "near neuro-vegetative state." According to sources cited in a recent article in the *Miami Herald*, Castro was having trouble speaking and remembering things; however, in a news piece by Paul Haven published later that month, Castro was alive and well. "I don't even remember what a headache feels like," Castro quipped in an article published about him entitled, "Fidel is Dying."

Possibly the many and varied reports of Castro's demise were pipe dreams of those who wanted him gone; perhaps he was in worse shape than he admitted.

In February 2013, a few short weeks before his good friend and mentee Hugo Chávez's death, Castro made his first public appearance in years, to vote in Cuba's public election. It wasn't easy for him, however. As he told reporters that had gathered around to take advantage of this rare appearance, "I asked various people who work with me the number of steps and the height of the stairway at the entrance. My shattered knee

. . . has taken its toll."

So why come out and vote at all? As Castro explained, it was important to show that their way worked, to not give in to another country's idea of successful government. Castro said, "The people are truly revolutionary; they have really sacrificed. We don't have to prove it; history will. Fifty years of the blockade and they haven't given in." And apparently, neither did Fidel.

CHAPTER THIRTY-FOUR

STEPPING DOWN

"My wishes have always been to discharge my duties to my last breath. That's all I can offer. But it would be a betrayal of my conscience to accept a responsibility requiring more mobility and dedication than I am physically able to offer. This I say devoid of all drama."

When Fidel Castro took over the Cuban government at barely 33 years of age, it was his intent to keep control of that government, to keep making advances and reforms for the Cuban people, until his last breath. Of course, for a young man who lived on the edge of battle and death, it was likely he never imagined he'd live so long, and could not possibly imagine the toll age would take on his body, and hence, his mind and his ability to rule in the manner he believed Cuba should be ruled.

On July 31, 2006, after his diagnosis of acute diverticulitis, he delegated his duties to Raul, naming him acting president while Fidel recovered. Fidel had no idea his recovery would take so long, however, and take so much out of him.

By February 2007, Fidel was not yet able to step back into

his leadership role, but was slowly starting to participate in government happenings again, though only to a point. Though even with his limited involvement, he knew he could never assume the full leadership reins again. On February 24, 2008, Raul became president, with Fidel as his main consult. Castro said, "I will not aspire to, neither will I accept—I repeat, I will not aspire to, neither will I accept—the position of president of the Council of State and commander in chief . . . It would betray my conscience to occupy a responsibility that requires mobility and the total commitment that I am not in the physical condition to offer."

Despite his diminished duties, Castro was realizing that he wasn't up to official government responsibility any more, and within a handful of years, he resigned his role of party leader of the Communist Party central committee also to Raul. Fidel Castro said, "I am not saying goodbye to you. I only wish to fight as a soldier of ideas." He continued to, as a figurehead, weigh in heavily on issues affecting Cuba and the world.

Still, after his resignation, he slowly stepped away, he says, "To prepare the people for my absence, psychologically and politically," explaining that this "was my first obligation after so many years of struggle."

In a letter to the people, Castro wrote, "This is not my farewell to you. My only wish is to fight as a soldier in the battle of ideas. I shall continue to write . . . Perhaps my voice will he heard . . . I shall be careful."

CHAPTER THIRTY-FIVE

CASTRO'S RETIREMENT

"I am someone who's been in politics for 43 years and I know what I'm doing and what I should do. Have no doubt that I know how to tell the truth and to do so elegantly."

While Fidel Castro officially stepped down and handed over the reins to brother Raul on July 31, 2006, after undergoing surgery for intestinal bleeding, he would not completely relinquish control for nearly two more years.

Castro said, "I believe that all of us ought to retire relatively young," but even into his eighties, he couldn't walk away from his work. By February of the following year, he was strong enough to start taking on other responsibilities, including becoming president of the Non-Aligned Movement during its 14th Summit, which had been held in Havana to appoint Castro for a term of one year.

Could Castro ever really walk away from being in power? It would seem he could not. "I can assure you that my first and foremost interest is my country. This is not a personal matter.

We are not people driven by a wish to be in the government since [it] is for us the least attractive work, even though we are politicians," he once said. In addition to being consulted on high-level government issues, he continued to interact with his countrymen and penned a regular column for *Granma* called "Reflections." He kept on top of world affairs and even maintained a Twitter account. But each year, he began letting go of more and more. On April 19, 2011, he formally resigned from the Communist Party.

Throughout his life, and even at the end of it, he maintained his deep Christianity, despite how he had been criticized for not practicing Christian ideals in his life and affairs. But he had his own take on it, saying, "If religious feeling is put in opposition to social change, then it does become an opium, but if it is joined to the struggle for social change, then it is a wonderful medicine." So even to his mind, he wasn't a textbook Catholic, but he believed devoutly in what he was doing—and believed it was deeper and more complex than typical religious belief. He said, "If people call me Christian, not from the standpoint of religion but from the standpoint of social vision, I declare that I am a Christian."

In 2014, he was awarded the Confucius Peace Prize, but he never let go of his distrust of the United States and his resistance of capitalist policies, though he continued to meet with world leaders from other countries.

Well before Barack Obama's March 2016 visit to Cuba, Castro was sharing his opinions on relations between Cuba and the U.S., and while he wasn't against Obama's visit, he did as early as January 2015 make his opinions known about what had come to be understood as the "Cuban Thaw," stating, in effect, that Cuba "has no need of gifts from the Empire."

In one of his last big public appearances in April 2015, he told the people that he knew he would die soon, but that communist ideals needed to live on.

CHAPTER THIRTY-SIX

THE CASTROS AND OBAMA

"Obama made a speech in which he uses the most sweetened words to express: 'It is time, now, to forget the past, leave the past behind, let us look to the future together, a future of hope. And it won't be easy, there will be challenges and we must give it time; but my stay here gives me more hope in what we can do together as friends, as family, as neighbors, together.' . . . I suppose all of us were at risk of a heart attack upon hearing these words from the President of the United States. After a ruthless blockade that has lasted almost 60 years, and what about those who have died in the mercenary attacks on Cuban ships and ports, an airliner full of passengers blown up in midair, mercenary invasions, multiple acts of violence and coercion?"

In March 2016, Barack Obama did something unprecedented for any American president for decades: He traveled to Havana to meet with leader Raul Castro in an attempt to begin to mend fences between the two countries.

During their fairly amicable news conference, the two

leaders lay their issues with each other out on the table and both seemed amenable to trying to work together. For Raul Castro, the most significant course of action the United States could take would be to lift the United States's trade embargo of Cuba, which Castro called "the most important obstacle to our economic development and the well-being of the Cuban people."

After Fidel Castro's passing, Obama made a statement that showed his respect for the work Castro had accomplished in his career, even if not in agreement. Said Obama:

"For nearly six decades, the relationship between the United States and Cuba was marked by discord and profound political disagreements. During my presidency, we have worked hard to put the past behind us, pursuing a future in which the relationship between our two countries is defined not by our differences but by the many things that we share as neighbors and friends—bonds of family, culture, commerce, and common humanity. This engagement includes the contributions of Cuban Americans, who have done so much for our country and who care deeply about their loved ones in Cuba."

It would be idealistic and even a little naïve to believe that Fidel Castro would have been in full support of Obama's assessment, when he always pointed out a fundamental disconnect between the way the U.S. and Cuba perceive the world. Castro had said, "North Americans don't understand . . . that our country is not just Cuba; our country is also humanity."

North Americans who are against Castro have certainly seen that differently than he did, though not all North Americans.

While he had seen promise in relations healing between Cuba and the United States during the Obama presidency, even asking his countrymen, "How can we help President Obama?" Fidel Castro's own words in his publication *Granma* following Obama's visit paint a more skeptical perspective. "We don't need the empire to give us anything," he wrote, even as his brother was open to discussing what an Obama-led American government could provide the people of Cuba, understanding "that a long and complex path still lies ahead" but that "what is most important is that we have started taking the first steps to build a new type of relationship, one that has never existed between Cuba and the United States."

That Obama did not meet with Fidel Castro during his March 2016 visit was not a slight on Fidel. For one, it was correct form for the leader to meet with the country's leader, Raul Castro. Also, Fidel's health had been steadily deteriorating since relinquishing his control of the country. Obama said, "If his health was good enough that I could meet with him, I'd be happy to meet with him, just as a symbol of the end of the—or, the closing of this Cold War chapter in our mutual histories."

How this new relationship will thrive or strain remains to be seen as Barack Obama is about to leave the office of the presidency and a less sympathetic president, Donald J. Trump, is about to take up where Obama left off. It's likely this new type of relationship will stall several more years before it can develop, or it will revert back to where it was when John F. Kennedy and Fidel Castro established the decades-long non-relationship between the countries.

Whatever happens, it will take time and perspective to fully realize Fidel Castro's ultimate impact on Cuba and the small nation's connection to the world. Said Barack Obama in his statement following Castro's death, "History will record and judge the enormous impact of this singular figure on the people and world around him."

But how would the death of *El Comandante* immediately impact the world?

CHAPTER THIRTY-SEVEN

THE FINAL FAREWELL

"[O]ur lives are but a fraction of a historical second, which must also be devoted in part to the vital necessities of every human being. One of the characteristics of this condition is the tendency to overvalue its role, in contrast, on the other hand, with the extraordinary number of persons who embody the loftiest dreams."

On November 25, 2016, Fidel Castro passed away peacefully at the age of 90. Raul Castro's announcement was greeted with mixed emotions around the world. Castro made a significant impact all over the world, over two centuries. While he is gone, that impact will live on.

Did anyone ever think the world would be free of him? He was certainly aware of how many enemies he had, and how hot a target he'd been for many governments and others. Did anyone, including Fidel, believe that death would come from natural causes?

In 1988, he quipped, "I think I hold the dubious record of having been the target of more assassination attempts than any politician, in any country, in any era . . . The day I die, nobody will believe it . . . If surviving assassination attempts were an Olympic event, I would win the gold medal." All told, Fidel Castro survived over 600 assassination attempts, according to Cuban officials.

He died as he lived: with no regrets. Castro has said, "I began revolution with 82 men. If I had to do it again, I'd do it with 10 or 15 and absolute faith. It does not matter how small you are if you have faith and plan of action."

The strong convictions from which he never wavered made him villain to most but a hero to many. One controversial set of comments came from Canadian Prime Minister Justin Trudeau. Upon learning of Fidel's passing, he made a statement expressing "deep sorrow" over the loss of ". . . a larger-than-life leader who served his people for almost half a century. A legendary revolutionary and orator, Mr. Castro made significant improvements to the education and health care of his island nation."

Many Americans were shocked and even angry at Trudeau's words, but for Trudeau, "I know my father [late Canadian Prime Minister Pierre Trudeau] was very proud to call him a friend and I had the opportunity to meet Fidel when my father passed away. It was also a real honor to meet his three sons and his brother President Raúl Castro during my recent visit to Cuba." Despite the common understanding that Canada has always had a friendlier relationship with the Castros and Cuba, the apparent admiration and even affection in his statement created an uproar for the young prime minister that doesn't show signs of cooling any time soon.

Like him or revile him, Castro made some incredible social strides for his country, though, perhaps in true socialist spirit, did not believe it was him, Fidel, that made these things happen. As he said, "Men do not shape destiny. Destiny produces the man for the hour."

He was in power nearly five decades. He outlasted 11 U.S. presidents. He created a system with free access to strong health care for all Cubans. Education is strong and also free. Castro has said that "even prostitutes have college degrees." Passing the baton to brother Raul was the first sign that he was ready; retiring from any role in government in 2008 was more telling. Castro said, "I think that a man should not live beyond the age when he begins to deteriorate, when the flame that lighted the brightest moment of his life has weakened."

In stark contrast to the remains of other communist dictators lying in state, Castro was cremated the day after his death, on Saturday, November 26, 2016, at his own request. "I'm not attached to anything," Castro said, and it makes sense that he would have chosen cremation. "I'm attached to what it feels it's my duty, to do my duty. I think that I will die with the boots on."

A national nine-day mourning period commenced following Castro's death, and his ashes were interred following a small private ceremony on Sunday, December 4, 2016.

How his revolution and the United States's recent friendly relations with Cuba will survive Fidel's mortality, however, remains to be seen.

CHAPTER THIRTY-EIGHT

CUBA AND THE U.S.: A SHAKY FUTURE

"With what moral authority can [the U.S.] speak of human rights . . . the rulers of a nation in which the millionaire and beggar coexist; where the Indian is exterminated; the black man is discriminated against; the woman is prostituted; and the great masses of Chicanos, Puerto Ricans, and Latin Americans are scorned, exploited, and humiliated . . . Where the CIA organizes plans of global subversion and espionage, and the Pentagon creates neutron bombs capable of preserving material assets and wiping out human beings."

While throughout his presidency, Barack Obama alluded to improving U.S. relations with Cuba, that may be coming to an end along with the end of his presidency. One imagines that a Hillary Clinton victory would have meant a continuation of the restorative work Obama began, but how a Trump administration might attack this initiative could be summed up in the attack Tweet Trump himself posted upon learning of Fidel Castro's death: "Fidel Castro is dead!"

A simple statement, made with enthusiasm, and the disdain further concretized in Trump's official statement, in which he explains that he will be rolling back any alliance-ship advances already made by the previous administration. "The world marks the passing of a brutal dictator who oppressed his own people for nearly six decades. Fidel Castro's legacy is one of firing squads, theft, unimaginable suffering, poverty, and the denial of fundamental human rights."

There hasn't been a discussion or meeting planned at the time of this writing between the leader of Cuba and the new leader of the Free World. There likely won't be.

Fidel Castro was not a supporter of American politics by and large, but he was always more receptive to American Democrats and Democratic policy. He actually made this statement in 2012, when Barack Obama ran for his second term against Mitt Romney: "The selection of a Republican candidate for the presidency of this globalized and expansive empire is—and I mean this seriously—the greatest competition of idiocy and ignorance that has ever been." He did not make a formal statement when the 2016 election went to the Republican candidate, though in his writings even weeks before his death, he appeared to support a Clinton presidency. "The first debate two weeks ago caused a stir. Mr. Trump, who presents himself as having expert ability, was left discredited as much as Barack (Obama) is in his policies."

One thing is fairly certain: If more work is going to be done to try to improve relations between the two nations, it's going to have to fall on two leaders who may not be all that interested in creating a friendly alliance—a fact on both sides of the divide. Fidel had said, "You Americans keep saying that Cuba is 90 miles from the United States. I say that the United States is 90 miles from Cuba and for us, that is worse." Both governments have each regarded the other as the enemy. What could cause this to change?

There have been small moments throughout the years where it seemed the two governments could make their peace. There was even a point where Castro made a comment that made capitalism think there was a victory. He said, "The Cuban model doesn't even work for us anymore," but he quickly backtracked on that, stating that any nation and economic system could use a change. He clarified his statement this way. "My idea, as the whole world knows, is that the capitalist system no longer works for the United States or the world. How could such a system work for a socialist country like Cuba?" The explanation doesn't quite align with the original statement, but for Castro, it was explanation enough.

Castro did not live in a bubble; he followed the state of American politics fairly closely. In fact, during Jeb Bush's run for the presidency, Castro made a comment about his weight. The criticism incited ire, which he smoothly and skillfully spoke to defect. "Forgive me for using the term 'fat little brother'" he said. "It is not a criticism, rather a suggestion that he do some exercises and go on a diet, don't you think? I'm doing this for the gentleman's health."

Likely he was doing it for both reasons, though he had long stood against people who criticize without action. Fidel has said, "All criticism is opposition. All opposition is counter-revolutionary." He has criticized the United States and capitalism the world over for doing exactly, ironically, what his critics have taken Fidel to task for: oppressing the masses. Fidel wondered:

> *"Why do some people have to go barefoot so that others can drive luxury cars? Why are some people able to live only 35 years in order that others can live 70 years? Why do some people have to be miserably poor in order that others can be extravagantly rich? I speak for all the children in the world who don't even have a piece of bread."*

For him, capitalism was the root of all evil, and that philosophy carries through in his legacy to Raul Castro and likely to the next head once Raul can no longer rule. Castro believed that capitalism took freedom and perspective away. Castro said, "A large percentage of those living in developed societies are told what brand of soda they should drink, what cigarettes they should smoke, what clothes and shoes they should wear, what they should eat and what brand of food they should buy. Their political ideas are supplied in the same way. Every year a trillion dollars is spent on advertising." For Castro, capitalism meant being fed what the government and business wanted you to eat. Interesting, as capitalism makes the same criticism of socialism and communism.

One of the more interesting differences between the Castro and staunch supporters of capitalism like Trump, however, is that Fidel Castro realized in his lifetime that it would be impossible to eradicate the planet of capitalism—and impossible for capitalism to overtake socialism without irreversible and even apocalyptic measures being put in place. Castro said, "I don't think that the contradictions between capitalism and socialism can be resolved by war. This is no longer the age of the bow and arrow. It's the nuclear age, and war can annihilate us all. The only way to achieve solutions seems to be for the different social systems to coexist."

Still, the effects of capitalism for the ones who were not "winning" at the game weighed heavily on Castro. "Nowhere in the world, in no act of genocide, in no war, are so many people killed per minute, per hour, and per day as those who are killed by hunger and poverty on our planet," he had said.

For all the criticisms of the Cuban government, the fact remains that the small island nation has made great strides in science and medical research, and strives to educate all of its citizens. In fact, the sense of impending climate danger is more widely held in Cuba than in the United States, and climate change has been a fundamental concern for Cuba for many years. Fidel also used climate change as a way to advance his own agenda, as he had believed, "The societies of consumption and squandering of material resources are incompatible with the idea of economic growth and a clean planet."

A big concern for Americans now is the feeling that First Amendment rights are going to be threatened by a new kind of administration, and anyone who fears that can side with Castro in why he believed so strongly in freedom of the press. Castro said, "The first thing dictators do is finish free press, to establish censorship. There is no doubt that a free press is the first enemy of dictatorship." It will be interesting to see how this will work itself out , and if the United States will be in the unique position of actually agreeing with Fidel Castro about something.

Another social issue that was important to Castro which may or may not still get the right kind of attention is how mental illness is handled in the United States. Said Castro, "The percentage of mentally disturbed people in the United States is very high. From the time the American gets up in the morning, he feels as if someone is trying to influence his will in some way; he is a person with a thousand pressures. The Americans live under a great strain . . . and have great feelings of frustration." For Castro, in explaining it this way, these illnesses are a direct result of the desire to have and consume as much as possible—the way of capitalism. Quickly put: Capitalism is crazy-making.

No surprises there. What will be surprising, however, in going forward in a world without Fidel Castro if his policies and practices become actively annihilated, if they passively break away due to neglect and disinterest, or if they find a way to morph into something less severe and more socially digestible—if the "good" he tried to do could actually find a way to get done.

For Fidel Castro, this would mean action, lots of continual action. Ideas are all well and good, but without people actually working to put those ideas into action, they are essentially useless. As Castro has said, "Whoever hesitates while waiting for ideas to triumph among the masses before initiating revolutionary action will never be a revolutionary. Humanity will, of course, change. Human society will, of course, continue to develop—in spite of men and the errors of men. But that is not a revolutionary attitude."

In Castro's mind, he wasn't ever a "bad" person. He was an agent of change. Being a revolutionary doesn't make a person evil—it makes them effective.

No matter what means he used to effect the change he needed to see, for him the destination far outweighed the journey, and the decisions and sacrifices—his own, or making others sacrifice—he made on the way to arrive where he needed to get, and to bring his country along with him, were all worth it in the end, because, in his mind, Cuba became a thriving utopia where science and social justice reigned supreme.

Late in his life, Castro was apologetic for at least one of his social misunderstandings. He believed that gays could be converted, and subjected many Cubans to horrible experiences of conversion. When he realized he was wrong, he owned it. "If someone is responsible, it's me," he said of that socially scarring snafu.

Whatever his legacy, it can't be denied that his impact was far-reaching and affecting, and will resonate for years to come.

EXCERPTS FROM
CASTRO'S SPEECHES

HISTORY WILL
ABSOLVE ME

Spoken in Santiago de Cuba
on October 16th, 1953.

Mark of Truth

I warn you, I am just beginning! If there is in your hearts
a vestige of love for your country, love for humanity, love for
justice, listen carefully. I know that I will be silenced for many
years; I know that the regime will try to suppress the truth
by all possible means; I know that there will be a conspiracy
to bury me in oblivion. But my voice will not be stifled—it
will rise from my breast even when I feel most alone, and
my heart will give it all the fire that callous cowards deny it.

From a shack in the mountains on Monday, July 27th, I listened to the dictator's voice on the air while there were still 18
of our men in arms against the government. Those who have
never experienced similar moments will never know that kind
of bitterness and indignation. While the long-cherished hopes
of freeing our people lay in ruins about us we heard those
crushed hopes gloated over by a tyrant more vicious, more
arrogant than ever. The endless stream of lies and slanders,
poured forth in his crude, odious, repulsive language, may

only be compared to the endless stream of clean young blood which had flowed since the previous night—with his knowledge, consent, complicity and approval—being spilled by the most inhuman gang of assassins it is possible to imagine. To have believed him for a single moment would have sufficed to fill a man of conscience with remorse and shame for the rest of his life. At that time, I could not even hope to brand his miserable forehead with the mark of truth which condemns him for the rest of his days and for all time to come. Already a circle of more than a thousand men, armed with weapons more powerful than ours and with peremptory orders to bring in our bodies, was closing in around us. Now that the truth is coming out, now that speaking before you I am carrying out the mission I set for myself, I may die peacefully and content. So, I shall not mince my words about those savage murderers.

A Worse Tyranny

Many decent military men are now asking themselves what need that Armed Forces had to assume the tremendous historical responsibility of destroying our Constitution merely to put a group of immoral men in power, men of bad reputation, corrupt, politically degenerate beyond redemption, who could never again have occupied a political post had it not been at bayonet-point; and they weren't even the ones with the bayonets in their hands . . .

On the other hand, the soldiers endure a worse tyranny than the civilians. They are under constant surveillance and not one of them enjoys the slightest security in his job. Any unjustified suspicion, any gossip, any intrigue, or denunciation, is sufficient to bring transfer, dishonorable discharge or imprisonment. Did not Tabernilla, in a memorandum, forbid them to talk with anyone opposed to the government, that is to say, with ninety-nine percent of the people? . . . What a lack of confidence! . . . Not even the vestal virgins of Rome had to abide by such a rule! As for the much-publicized little houses for enlisted men, there aren't 300 on the whole Island; yet with what has been spent on tanks, guns and other weaponry every soldier might have a place to live. Batista isn't concerned with taking care of the Army, but that the Army take care of him! He increases the Army's power of oppression and killing but does not improve living conditions for the soldiers. Triple guard duty, constant confinement to barracks, continuous anxiety, the enmity of the people, uncertainty about the future—this is what has been given to the soldier. In other words: "Die for the regime, soldier, give it your sweat and blood. We shall dedicate a speech to you and award you a posthumous promotion (when it no longer matters) and afterwards . . . we shall go on living luxuriously, making ourselves rich. Kill, abuse, oppress the people. When the people get tired and all this comes to an end, you can pay for our crimes while we go abroad and live like kings. And if one day we return, don't you or your children knock on the doors of our mansions, for we shall be millionaires and millionaires do not mingle with the poor. Kill, soldier, oppress the people, die for the regime, give your sweat and blood . . ."

But if blind to this sad truth, a minority of soldiers had decided to fight the people, the people who were going to liberate them from tyranny, victory still would have gone to the people. The Honorable Prosecutor was very interested in knowing our chances for success. These chances were based on considerations of technical, military and social order. They have tried to establish the myth that modern arms render the people helpless in overthrowing tyrants. Military parades and the pompous display of machines of war are used to perpetuate this myth and to create a complex of absolute impotence in the people. But no weaponry, no violence can vanquish the people once they are determined to win back their rights. Both past and present are full of examples. The most recent is the revolt in Bolivia, where miners with dynamite sticks smashed and defeated regular army regiments.

Fortunately, we Cubans need not look for examples abroad. No example is as inspiring as that of our own land. During the war of 1895 there were nearly half a million armed Spanish soldiers in Cuba, many more than the Dictator counts upon today to hold back a population five times greater. The arms of the Spaniards were, incomparably, both more up to date and more powerful than those of our mambises. Often the Spaniards were equipped with field artillery and the infantry used breechloaders similar to those still in use by the infantry of today. The Cubans were usually armed with no more than their machetes, for their cartridge belts were almost always empty. There is an unforgettable passage in the history of our War of Independence, narrated by General Miró Argenter, Chief of Antonio Maceo's General Staff. I managed to bring it copied on this scrap of paper so I wouldn't have to depend upon my memory:

"Untrained men under the command of Pedro Delgado, most of them equipped only with machetes, were virtually annihilated as they threw themselves on the solid rank of Spaniards. It is not an exaggeration to assert that of every fifty men, 25 were killed. Some even attacked the Spaniards with their bare fists, without machetes, without even knives. Searching through the reeds by the Hondo River, we found 15 more dead from the Cuban party, and it was not immediately clear what group they belonged to. They did not appear to have shouldered arms, their clothes were intact and only tin drinking cups hung from their waists; a few steps further on lay the dead horse, all its equipment in order. We reconstructed the climax of the tragedy. These men, following their daring chief, Lieutenant Colonel Pedro Delgado, had earned heroes' laurels: they had thrown themselves against bayonets with bare hands, the clash of metal which was heard around them was the sound of their drinking cups banging against the saddle horn. Maceo was deeply moved. This man so used to seeing death in all its forms murmured this praise: 'I had never seen anything like this, untrained and unarmed men attacking the Spaniards with only drinking cups for weapons. And I called it impedimenta!'"

This is how peoples fight when they want to win their freedom; they throw stones at airplanes and overturn tanks!

As soon as Santiago de Cuba was in our hands we would immediately have readied the people of Oriente for war. Bayamo was attacked precisely to locate our advance forces along the Cauto River. Never forget that this province, which has a million and a half inhabitants today, is the most rebellious and patriotic in Cuba. It was this province that sparked the fight for independence for thirty years and paid the highest price in blood, sacrifice and heroism. In Oriente you can still breathe the air of that glorious epic. At dawn, when the cocks crow as if they were bugles calling soldiers to reveille, and when the sun rises radiant over the rugged mountains, it seems that once again we will live the days of Yara or Baire!

I stated that the second consideration on which we based our chances for success was one of social order. Why were we sure of the people's support? When we speak of the people we are not talking about those who live in comfort, the conservative elements of the nation, who welcome any repressive regime, any dictatorship, any despotism, prostrating themselves before the masters of the moment until they grind their foreheads into the ground. When we speak of struggle and we mention the people we mean the vast unredeemed masses, those to whom everyone makes promises and who are deceived by all; we mean the people who yearn for a better, more dignified and more just nation; who are moved by ancestral aspirations to justice, for they have suffered injustice and mockery generation after generation; those who long for great and wise changes in all aspects of their life; people who, to attain those changes, are ready to give even the very last breath they have when they believe in something or in someone, especially when they believe in themselves. The first condition of sincerity and good faith in any endeavor is to do precisely what nobody else ever does, that is, to speak with absolute clarity, without fear. The demagogues and professional politicians who manage to perform the miracle of being right about everything and of pleasing everyone are, necessarily, deceiving everyone about everything. The revolutionaries must proclaim their ideas courageously, define their principles and express their intentions so that no one is deceived, neither friend nor foe.

In terms of struggle, when we talk about people we're talking about the six hundred thousand Cubans without work, who want to earn their daily bread honestly without having to emigrate from their homeland in search of a livelihood; the five hundred thousand farm laborers who live in miserable shacks, who work four months of the year and starve the rest, sharing their misery with their children, who don't have an inch of land to till and whose existence would move any heart not made of stone; the four hundred thousand industrial workers and laborers whose retirement funds have been embezzled, whose benefits are being taken away, whose homes are wretched quarters, whose salaries pass from the hands of the boss to those of the moneylender, whose future is a pay reduction and dismissal, whose life is endless work and whose only rest is the tomb; the one hundred thousand small farmers who live and die working land that is not theirs, looking at it with the sadness of Moses gazing at the promised land, to die without ever owning it, who like feudal serfs have to pay for the use of their parcel of land by giving up a portion of its produce, who cannot love it, improve it, beautify it nor plant a cedar or an orange tree on it because they never know when a sheriff will come with the rural guard to evict them from it; the thirty thousand teachers and professors who are so devoted, dedicated and so necessary to the better destiny of future generations and who are so badly treated and paid; the 20 thousand small business men weighed down by debts, ruined by the crisis and harangued by a plague of grafting and venal officials; the ten thousand young professional people: doctors, engineers, lawyers, veterinarians, school teachers, dentists, pharmacists, newspapermen, painters, sculptors, etc., who finish school with their degrees anxious to work and full of hope, only to find themselves at a dead end, all doors closed to them, and where no ears hear their clamor or supplication. These are the people, the ones who know misfortune and, therefore, are capable of fighting with limitless courage! To these people whose desperate roads through life have been paved with the bricks of betrayal and false promises, we were not going to say: "We will give you . . ." but rather: "Here it is, now fight for it with everything you have, so that liberty and happiness may be yours!"

Cuba's Six Problems

The problem of the land, the problem of industrialization, the problem of housing, the problem of unemployment, the problem of education and the problem of the people's health: these are the six problems we would take immediate steps to solve, along with restoration of civil liberties and political democracy.

This exposition may seem cold and theoretical if one does not know the shocking and tragic conditions of the country with regard to these six problems, along with the most humiliating political oppression.

Eighty-five per cent of the small farmers in Cuba pay rent and live under constant threat of being evicted from the land they till. More than half of our most productive land is in the hands of foreigners. In Oriente, the largest province, the lands of the United Fruit Company and the West Indian Company link the northern and southern coasts. There are two hundred thousand peasant families who do not have a single acre of land to till to provide food for their starving children. On the other hand, nearly three hundred thousand caballerías of cultivable land owned by powerful interests remain uncultivated. If Cuba is above all an agricultural State, if its population is largely rural, if the city depends on these rural areas, if the people from our countryside won our war of independence, if our nation's greatness and prosperity depend on a healthy and vigorous rural population that loves the land and knows how to work it, if this population depends on a State that protects and guides it, then how can the present state of affairs be allowed to continue?

Except for a few food, lumber and textile industries, Cuba continues to be primarily a producer of raw materials. We export sugar to import candy, we export hides to import shoes, we export iron to import plows . . . Everyone agrees with the urgent need to industrialize the nation, that we need steel industries, paper and chemical industries, that we must improve our cattle and grain production, the technology and processing in our food industry in order to defend ourselves against the ruinous competition from Europe in cheese products, condensed milk, liquors and edible oils, and the United States in canned goods; that we need cargo ships; that tourism should be an enormous source of revenue. But the capitalists insist that the workers remain under the yoke. The State sits back with its arms crossed and industrialization can wait forever.

Just as serious or even worse is the housing problem. There are two hundred thousand huts and hovels in Cuba; four hundred thousand families in the countryside and in the cities live cramped in huts and tenements without even the minimum sanitary requirements; two million two hundred thousand of our urban population pay rents which absorb between one fifth and one third of their incomes; and two million eight hundred thousand of our rural and suburban population lack electricity. We have the same situation here: if the State proposes the lowering of rents, landlords threaten to freeze all construction; if the State does not interfere, construction goes on so long as landlords get high rents; otherwise they would not lay a single brick even though the rest of the population had to live totally exposed to the elements. The utilities monopoly is no better; they extend lines as far as it is profitable and beyond that point they don't care if people have to live in darkness for the rest of their lives. The State sits back with its arms crossed and the people have neither homes nor electricity.

Our educational system is perfectly compatible with everything I've just mentioned. Where the peasant doesn't own the land, what need is there for agricultural schools? Where there is no industry, what need is there for technical or vocational schools? Everything follows the same absurd logic; if we don't have one thing we can't have the other. In any small European country, there are more than 200 technological and vocational schools; in Cuba only six such schools exist, and their graduates have no jobs for their skills. The little rural schoolhouses are attended by a mere half of the school age children—barefooted, half-naked and undernourished—and frequently the teacher must buy necessary school materials from his own salary. Is this the way to make a nation great?

Only death can liberate one from so much misery. In this respect, however, the State is most helpful—in providing early death for the people. Ninety per cent of the children in the countryside are consumed by parasites which filter through their bare feet from the ground they walk on. Society is moved to compassion when it hears of the kidnapping or murder of one child, but it is indifferent to the mass murder of so many thousands of children who die every year from lack of facilities, agonizing with pain. Their innocent eyes, death already shining in them, seem to look into some vague infinity as if entreating forgiveness for human selfishness, as if asking God to stay His wrath. And when the head of a family works only four months a year, with what can he purchase clothing and medicine for his children? They will grow up with rickets, with not a single good tooth in their mouths by the time they reach thirty; they will have heard ten million speeches and will finally die of misery and deception. Public hospitals, which are always full, accept only patients recommended by some powerful politician who, in return, demands the votes of the unfortunate one and his family so that Cuba may continue forever in the same or worse condition.

The Fraternity of the Rich

With this background, is it not understandable that from May to December over a million persons are jobless and that Cuba, with a population of five and a half million, has a greater number of unemployed than France or Italy with a population of forty million each?

When you try a defendant for robbery, Honorable Judges, do you ask him how long he has been unemployed? Do you ask him how many children he has, which days of the week he ate and which he didn't, do you investigate his social context at all? You just send him to jail without further thought. But those who burn warehouses and stores to collect insurance do not go to jail, even though a few human beings may have gone up in flames. The insured have money to hire lawyers and bribe judges. You imprison the poor wretch who steals because he is hungry; but none of the hundreds who steal millions from the Government has ever spent a night in jail. You dine with them at the end of the year in some elegant club and they enjoy your respect. In Cuba, when a government official becomes a millionaire overnight and enters the fraternity of the rich, he could very well be greeted with the words of that opulent character out of Balzac—Taillefer—who in his toast to the young heir to an enormous fortune, said: "Gentlemen, let us drink to the power of gold! Mr. Valentine, a millionaire six times over, has just ascended the throne. He is king, can do everything, is above everyone, as all the rich are. Henceforth, equality before the law, established by the Constitution, will be a myth for him; for he will not be subject to laws: the laws will be subject to him. There are no courts nor are there sentences for millionaires."

The nation's future, the solutions to its problems, cannot continue to depend on the selfish interests of a dozen big businessmen nor on the cold calculations of profits that ten or twelve magnates draw up in their air-conditioned offices. The country cannot continue begging on its knees for miracles from a few golden calves, like the Biblical one destroyed by the prophet's fury. Golden calves cannot perform miracles of any kind. The problems of the Republic can be solved only if we dedicate ourselves to fight for it with the same energy, honesty and patriotism our liberators had when they founded it.

A Revolutionary Government

In this present-day world, social problems are not solved by spontaneous generation.

A revolutionary government backed by the people and with the respect of the nation, after cleansing the different institutions of all venal and corrupt officials, would proceed immediately to the country's industrialization, mobilizing all inactive capital, currently estimated at about 1.5 billion pesos, through the National Bank and the Agricultural and Industrial Development Bank, and submitting this mammoth task to experts and men of absolute competence totally removed from all political machines for study, direction, planning and realization.

After settling the one hundred thousand small farmers as owners on the land which they previously rented, a revolutionary government would immediately proceed to settle the land problem. First, as set forth in the Constitution, it would establish the maximum amount of land to be held by each type of agricultural enterprise and would acquire the excess acreage by expropriation, recovery of swampland, planting of large nurseries, and reserving of zones for reforestation. Secondly, it would distribute the remaining land among peasant families with priority given to the larger ones, and would promote agricultural cooperatives for communal use of expensive equipment, freezing plants and unified professional technical management of farming and cattle raising. Finally, it would provide resources, equipment, protection and useful guidance to the peasants.

A revolutionary government would solve the housing

problem by cutting all rents in half, by providing tax exemptions on homes inhabited by the owners; by tripling taxes on rented homes; by tearing down hovels and replacing them with modern apartment buildings; and by financing housing all over the island on a scale heretofore unheard of, with the criterion that, just as each rural family should possess its own tract of land, each city family should own its own house or apartment. There is plenty of building material and more than enough manpower to make a decent home for every Cuban. But if we continue to wait for the golden calf, a thousand years will have gone by and the problem will remain the same. On the other hand, today possibilities of taking electricity to the most isolated areas on the island are greater than ever. The use of nuclear energy in this field is now a reality and will greatly reduce the cost of producing electricity.

With these three projects and reforms, the problem of unemployment would automatically disappear and the task of improving public health and fighting against disease would become much less difficult.

Finally, a revolutionary government would undertake the integral reform of the educational system, bringing it into line with the projects just mentioned with the idea of educating those generations which will have the privilege of living in a happier land. Do not forget the words of the Apostle: "A grave mistake is being made in Latin America: in countries that live almost completely from the produce of the land, men are being educated exclusively for urban life and are not trained for farm life." "The happiest country is the one which has best educated its sons, both in the instruction of thought and the direction of their feelings." "An educated country will always be strong and free."

The soul of education, however, is the teacher, and in Cuba the teaching profession is miserably underpaid. Despite this, no one is more dedicated than the Cuban teacher. Who among us has not learned his three Rs in the little public schoolhouse? It is time we stopped paying pittances to these young men and women who are entrusted with the sacred task of teaching our youth. No teacher should earn less than 200 pesos, no secondary teacher should make less than 350 pesos, if they are to devote themselves exclusively to their high calling without suffering want. What is more, all rural teachers should have free use of the various systems of transportation; and, at least once every five years, all teachers should enjoy a sabbatical leave of six months with pay so they may attend special refresher courses at home or abroad to keep abreast of the latest developments in their field. In this way, the curriculum and the teaching system can be easily improved. Where will the money be found for all this? When there is an end to the embezzlement of government funds, when public officials stop taking graft from the large companies that owe taxes to the State, when the enormous resources of the country are brought into full use, when we no longer buy tanks, bombers and guns for this country (which has no frontiers to defend and where these instruments of war, now being purchased, are used against the people), when there is more interest in educating the people than in killing them there will be more than enough money.

Cuba could easily provide for a population three times as great as it has now, so there is no excuse for the abject poverty of a single one of its present inhabitants. The markets should be overflowing with produce, pantries should be full, all hands should be working. This is not an inconceivable thought. What is inconceivable is that anyone should go to bed hungry while there is a single inch of unproductive land; that children should die for lack of medical attention; what is inconceivable is that 30% of our farm people cannot write their names and that 99% of them know nothing of Cuba's history. What is inconceivable is that the majority of our rural people are now living in worse circumstances than the Indians Columbus discovered in the fairest land that human eyes had ever seen.

To those who would call me a dreamer, I quote the words of Martí: "A true man does not seek the path where advantage lies, but rather the path where duty lies, and this is the only practical man, whose dream of today will be the law of tomorrow, because he who has looked back on the essential course of history and has seen flaming and bleeding peoples seethe in the cauldron of the ages knows that, without a single exception, the future lies on the side of duty."

Only when we understand that such a high ideal inspired them can we conceive of the heroism of the young men who fell in Santiago. The meager material means at our disposal was all that prevented sure success.

History Will Absolve Me

Still there is one argument more powerful than all the others. We are Cubans and to be Cuban implies a duty; not to fulfill that duty is a crime, is treason. We are proud of the history of our country; we learned it in school and have grown up hearing of freedom, justice and human rights. We were taught to venerate the glorious example of our heroes and martyrs. Céspedes, Agramonte, Maceo, Gómez and Martí were the first names engraved in our minds. We were taught that the Titan once said that liberty is not begged for but won with the blade of a machete. We were taught that for the guidance of Cuba's free citizens, the Apostle wrote in his book The Golden Age: "The man who abides by unjust laws and permits any man to trample and mistreat the country in which he was born is not an honorable man . . . In the world, there must be a certain degree of honor just as there must be a certain amount of light. When there are many men without honor, there are always others who bear in themselves the honor of many men. These are the men who rebel with great force against those who steal the people's freedom, that is to say, against those who steal honor itself. In those men thousands more are contained, an entire people is contained, human dignity is contained . . ." We were taught that the 10th of October and the 24th of February are glorious anniversaries of national rejoicing because they mark days on which Cubans rebelled against the yoke of infamous tyranny. We were taught to cherish and defend the beloved flag of the lone star, and to sing every afternoon the verses of our National Anthem: "To live in chains is to live in disgrace and in opprobrium," and "to die for one's homeland is to live forever!" All this we learned and will never forget, even though today in our land there is murder and prison for the men who practice the ideas taught to them since the cradle. We were born in a free country that our parents bequeathed to us, and the Island will first sink into the sea before we consent to be the slaves of anyone.

It seemed that the Apostle would die during his Centennial.

It seemed that his memory would be extinguished forever. So great was the affront! But he is alive; he has not died. His people are rebellious. His people are worthy. His people are faithful to his memory. There are Cubans who have fallen defending his doctrines. There are young men who in magnificent selflessness came to die beside his tomb, giving their blood and their lives so that he could keep on living in the heart of his nation. Cuba, what would have become of you had you let your Apostle die?

I come to the close of my defense plea but I will not end it as lawyers usually do, asking that the accused be freed. I cannot ask freedom for myself while my comrades are already suffering in the ignominious prison of the Isle of Pines. Send me there to join them and to share their fate. It is understandable that honest men should be dead or in prison in a Republic where the President is a criminal and a thief.

To you, Honorable Judges, my sincere gratitude for having allowed me to express myself free from contemptible restrictions. I hold no bitterness towards you, I recognize that in certain aspects you have been humane, and I know that the Chief Judge of this Court, a man of impeccable private life, cannot disguise his repugnance at the current state of affairs that compels him to dictate unjust decisions. Still, a more serious problem remains for the Court of Appeals: the indictments arising from the murders of seventy men, that is to say, the greatest massacre we have ever known. The guilty continue at liberty and with weapons in their hands—weapons which continually threaten the lives of all citizens. If all the weight of the law does not fall upon the guilty because of cowardice or because of domination of the courts, and if then all the judges do not resign, I pity your honor. And I regret the unprecedented shame that will fall upon the Judicial Power.

I know that imprisonment will be harder for me than it has ever been for anyone, filled with cowardly threats and hideous cruelty. But I do not fear prison, as I do not fear the fury of the miserable tyrant who took the lives of 70 of my comrades. Condemn me. It does not matter. History will absolve me.

TO THE U.N. GENERAL ASSEMBLY: THE PROBLEM OF CUBA AND ITS REVOLUTIONARY POLICY

Spoken in Washington, DC
on September 26th, 1960.

Mr. President,
Fellow Delegates

Although it has been said of us that we speak at great length, you may rest assured that we shall endeavor to be brief and to put before you what we consider it our duty to say. We shall also speak slowly in order to co-operate with the interpreters.

Some people may think that we are very annoyed and upset by the treatment the Cuban delegation has received. This is not the case. We understand full well the reasons behind it. That is why we are not irritated. Nor should anybody worry that Cuba will not continue to the effort of achieving a world-wide understanding. That being so, we shall speak openly.

It is extremely expensive to send a delegation to the United Nations. We, the underdeveloped countries, do not have many resources to spend, unless it is to speak openly at this meeting of representatives of almost every country in the world.

The speakers who have preceded me on this rostrum have expressed their concern about problems the whole world is concerned about. We too are concerned about those problems and yet, in the case of Cuba, there is a very special circumstance, and it is that, at this moment, Cuba itself must be a concern for the world, because, as several delegates have rightly said here, among the many current problems of the world, there is the problem of Cuba. In addition to the problems facing the world today, Cuba has problems of her own, problems which worry her people.

A World of Monopolies

The case of Cuba is not isolated case. It would be an error to think of it only as the case of Cuba. The case of Cuba is the case of all underdeveloped countries. The case of Cuba is like that of the Congo, Egypt, Algeria, Iran. . . (APPLAUSE) . . . like that of Panama, which wishes to have its canal; it is like that of Puerto Rico, whose national spirit they are destroying; like that of Honduras, a portion of whose territory has been alienated. In short, although we have not make specific reference to other countries, the case of Cuba is the case of all underdeveloped, colonialized countries.

The problems which we have been describing in relation to Cuba can be applied just as well to all of Latin America. The control of Latin American economic resources by the monopolies, which, when they do not own the mines directly and are in charge of extraction, as the case with the copper of Chile, Peru, or Mexico, and with the oil of Venezuela—

when this control is not exercised directly it is because they are the owners of the public utility companies, as is the case in Argentina, Brazil, Chile, Peru, Ecuador and Colombia, or the owners of telephone services, which is the case in Chile, Brazil, Peru, Venezuela, Paraguay and Bolivia, or they commercialize our products, as is the case with coffee in Brazil, Colombia, El Salvador, Costa Rica, and Guatemala, or with the cultivation, marketing and transportations of bananas by the United Fruit Co. in Guatemala, Costa Rica, and Honduras, or with the Cotton in Mexico and Brazil. In other words, the monopolies control the most important industries. Woe to those countries, the day they try to make an agrarian reform! They will be asked for immediate, efficient, and just payment. And if, in spite of everything they make an agrarian reform, the representative of the friendly country who comes to the United Nations will be confined to Manhattan; they will not rent hotel space to him; insult will he heaped upon him, and it is even possible that he may be physically mistreated by the police.

The problem of Cuba is just an example of the situation in Latin America. And how long will Latin America wait for its development? It will have to wait, according to the point of view of the monopolies, until there are two Fridays in a week.

Who is going to industrialize Latin America? The monopolies? Certainly not. There is a report by the economic Commission of the United Nations which explains how private capital, instead of going to the countries that need it most for the establishment of basic industries to contribute to their development, is being channeled referentially to the more industrialized countries, because there, according to their beliefs, private capital finds greater security. And, of course, even the Economic Secretariat of the United Nations has had to admit there is no possible chance for development through the investment of private capital—that is, through the monopolies.

The development of Latin America will have to be achieved through public investment, planned and granted unconditionally without any political strings attached, because, naturally, we all like to be representatives of free countries. None of us like to represent a country that does not feel itself in full possession of its freedom.

None of us wants the independence of this country to be subjected to any interest other than that of the country itself. That is why assistance must be given without any political conditions.

That help has been denied to us does not matter. We have not asked for it. However, in the interest of and for the benefit of the Latin American peoples, we do feel duty bound out of solidarity, to stress the fact that the assistance must be given without any political conditions whatsoever. There should be more public investments for economic development, rather than for "social development," which is the latest thing invented to hide the true need for the economic development of countries.

The problems of Latin America are similar to those of the rest of the world: to those of Africa and Asia. The world is divided up among the monopolies; the same monopolies that we find in Latin America are also found in the Middle East. There the oil is in the hands of monopolistic companies that are controlled by France, the United States, the United

Kingdom the Netherlands . . . in Iran, Iraq, Saudi Arabia, Kuwait, in short, in all corners of the world. The same thing is true, for instance, in the Philippines, and in Africa. The world has been divided among the monopolistic interests. Who would dare deny this historic truth? The monopolistic interests do not want to see the development of countries and the people themselves. And the sooner they recover or amortize the capital invested, the better.

The Business of War

And, above all, if we, the underdeveloped countries, want to preserve the hope of achieving progress, if we want to have a chance of seeing our peoples enjoying a higher standard of living, let us struggle for peace, let us struggle for disarmament; with a fifth of what the world spends on armaments, we could promote the development of all the underdeveloped countries at a rate of growth of 10 percent per annum. With a fifth of the resources which countries spend on armaments, we could surely raise the people's standard of living.

Now, what are the obstacles to disarmament? Who is interested in being armed? Those who are interested in being armed to the teeth are those who want to keep colonies, those who want to maintain their monopolies, those who want to retain control of the oil of the Middle East; the natural resources of Latin America, of Asia, of Africa, and who require military strength to defend their interests. And it is well known that these territories were occupied and colonized on the strength of the law of force; by virtue of the law of force millions of men were enslaved, and it is force which sustains such exploitation in the world. Therefore, those who want no disarmament are those interested in maintaining their military strength in order to retain control of natural resources, the wealth of the people of the world, and cheap labor in underdeveloped countries. We promised to speak openly, and there is no other way of telling the truth.

The colonialists, therefore, are against disarmament. Using the weapon of world public opinion, we must fight to force disarmament on them as we must force them to respect the right of peoples to economic and political liberation.

The monopolies are against disarmament, because, besides being able to defend those interests with arms, the arms race has always been good business for them. For example, it is well known that the great monopolies in this country doubled their capital shortly after the Second World War. Like vultures, the monopolies feed on the corpses which are the harvest of war.

And war is a business. Those who trade in war, those who enrich themselves in war, must be unmasked. We must open the eyes of the world and expose those who trade in the destiny of mankind, in the danger of war, particularly when the war may be so frightful that it leaves no hope of salvation.

We, the small and underdeveloped countries, urge the whole Assembly and especially the other small and underdeveloped nations to devote themselves to this task and to have this problem discussed here, because afterwards we will never forgive ourselves if, through our neglect or lack of firmness and energy on this basic issue, the world becomes involved once again in the perils of war.

The Cuban Position

We know well what will be said about us, today, tomorrow, every day, to deceive the American people. But is does not matter. We are doing our duty by stating our views in, this historic Assembly.

We proclaim the right of people to freedom, the right of people to nationhood; those who know that nationalism means the desire of the people to regain what is rightly theirs, their wealth, their natural resources, conspire against nationalism.

We are, in short, for all the noble aspirations of all the peoples. That is our position. We are, and always shall be for everything that is just: against colonialism, exploitation, monopolies, militarism, the armaments race, and warmongering. We shall always be against such things. That will be our position.

. . . . Some people wanted to know what the policy of the Revolutionary Government of Cuba was. Very well, then, this is our policy (OVATION).

MAY DAY CELEBRATION: CUBA IS A SOCIALIST NATION

Spoken in Havana, Cuba on May 2nd, 1961.

The Fruits of the Revolution

We have been witnesses, all of us Cubans, of every step taken by the revolution, so maybe we cannot realize how much we have advanced as fully as can be understood by visitors, particularly those visitors from Latin America, where today they are still living in a world very similar to the one we lived in yesterday. It is as if they were suddenly transported from the past to the present of our revolution, with all its extraordinary progress as compared to the past. We do not intend tonight to stress the merit of what we have done. We merely want to locate ourselves at the point where we are at the present.

We had a chance today to see genuine results of the revolution on this May Day, so different from the May Days of the past. Formerly that date was the occasion for each sector of labor to set forth its demands, its aspirations for improvement, to men who were deaf to the working-class interests, men who could not even accede to those basic demands because they did not govern for the people, for the workers, for the peasants, or for the humble; they governed solely for the privileged, the dominant economic interests. Doing anything for the people would have meant harming the interests that they represented, and so they could not accede to any just demand from the people. The May Day parades of those days marked the complaints and protest of the workers.

How different today's parade has been! How different even from the first parades after the revolution triumphed. Today's parade shows us how much we have advanced. The workers (Light applause) now do not have to submit themselves to those trials; the workers now do not have to implore deaf executives; the workers now are not subject to the domination of any

exploiting class; the workers no longer live in a country run by men serving exploiting interests. The workers know now that everything the revolution does, everything the government does or can do, has one goal: helping the workers, helping the people. (Applause)

Otherwise, there would be no explanation for the spontaneous sentiment of support for the Revolutionary Government, that overflowing good will that every man and woman has expressed today. (Applause)

Fruits of the revolution are seen everywhere. The first to parade today were the children of the Camilo Cienfuegos school center. We saw the Pioneers parade by with the smile of hope, confidence, and affection. We saw the young rebels parade by. We saw the women of the federation go by. We saw children from numberless schools created by the revolution parade.

We saw 1,000 students from the 600 sugar-cane cooperatives who are studying artificial insemination here in the capital. We saw young people, humble people, parade with their uniforms of the school center where they are learning to be diplomatic representatives of the future.

We saw the pupils of the schools for young peasants of the Zapata swamps parade by, the swamps that the mercenaries chose for their attack. We saw thousands and thousands of peasants who are studying in the capital and who come from distant mountain areas or from cane cooperatives or from people's farms parade. We saw the young girls studying for children's club work. And here every one of these groups staged scenes that are worthy of praise. And we saw also what is going into the rural areas. The volunteer teachers paraded and also representatives of the 100,000 young people on their way to the interior to wipe out illiteracy. Where does this strength come from? It comes from the people, and it is devoted to the people in return.

These young people are truly children of the people. When we saw them today writing "Long Live Our Socialist Revolution" with their formations we though how hard it would have been to have all this without a revolution; how hard for any of these children from the mountains to have paraded here today, or any of these young people from the rural areas to have a chance to get to know the capital, or to study in any of these schools, or to parade with the joy and pride shown here today, or to march with the faith in the future shown today, because schools, university professions, art, culture, and honors were never for the children of poor families, in town or in the country. They were never for the peasant of the remote rural areas; they were never for the poor young fellow, black or white, or our countryside and cities.

Art, culture, university professions, opportunities, honors, elegant clothes were only the privilege of a small minority, a minority represented today with that grace and humor shown by some worker federations in their imitations of the rich. It is astounding to think that today more than 20,000 athletes paraded. if one remembers that we are just beginning. And this, without touching on the most marvelous thing we had a chance to see today, that is, this armed nation, this united people, which came to attend these ceremonies.

How would it have been possible without a revolution? How can one compare this present with the past? How can one avoid emotion on seeing endless lines of workers, athletes, and militiamen parade by. At times, all went to intermingled. After all, workers, athletes, and soldiers are the same thing. Anybody could understand why our people, must emerge victorious in any battle. We noted the many women in the ranks of the federations. The men were in the artillery units, mortar units, ack-ack units, or militia battalions. The women were the wives and sisters and sweethearts of the militiamen who marched by later in the battalions and those young men of the basic secondary schools, the Pioneers who paraded by were their sons.

And so, one can see today the unity of the humble people who are fighting for the poor. Workers of every profession; manual laborers and intellectual workers; all were marching together, the writer, artist, actor, announcer, doctor, nurse, clinical employer. Marching together in great numbers under the flag of the national education workers' union were the teachers, employees of the Education Ministry. (Applause).

The Duty to Work

Today we have had a chance to see everything worthwhile in our country, everything produced in our country. We have understood better than ever that there are two classes of citizens, or rather there were two classes of citizens; the citizens who worked, produced, and created and the citizens who lived without working or producing. These latter were parasites.

(Applause)

In this young, fervent nation, who did not parade today, who could not parade here today? The parasites! Today the working people paraded, everybody who produces with his hands or his brain. I do not mean that workers who did not have a chance to parade were parasites, because they had to take care of their children, or were ill, or even just did not want to parade today. I am speaking only of those who were not represented here because they could not be represented by those who produce.

This is the people, the true people. He who lives as a parasite does not belong to the people. Only the invalid, the sick, the old, the children are entitled to live without working and are entitled to have us work for them and to care for them, and from the work of everyone they can be benefited. For the children, the old, the invalid, and the sick, we have the duty to work, all of us. (Applause) What no moral law will be able to justify ever is for the people to work for the parasites. (Applause)

Those who paraded today were the working people who will

never resign themselves to work for the parasites. (Applause) In this manner our national community has understood what the revolution is, and has understood clearly what the meaning of a revolution is in which a nation gets rid of parasites from the outside and those inside. (Applause) We remember that because of the nationalization of the largest industries of the nation, and just before the U.S. factories were nationalized, some asked: Was not this factory a Cuban factory? Why should a Cuban factory be nationalized? Well, such a factory did not belong to the people, it belonged to some man. Now they belong to the nation. (Applause)

No Threat to the U.S.

The U.S. Government says that a socialist regime here threatens U.S. security. But what threatens the security of the North American people is the aggressive policy of the warmongers of the United States. What threatens the security of the North American family and people is the violence, that aggressive policy, that policy that ignores the sovereignty and the rights of other peoples. The one who is threatening the security of the United States is Kennedy, with that aggressive policy. That aggressive policy can give rise to a world war; and that world war can cost the lives of tens of millions of North Americans. Therefore, the one who threatens the security of the United States is not the Cuban Revolutionary Government but the aggressor and aggressive government of the United States.

We do not endanger the security of a single North American. We do not endanger the life or security of a single North American family. We, making cooperatives, agrarian reform, people's ranches, houses, schools, literacy campaigns, and sending thousands and thousands of teachers to the interior, building hospitals, sending doctors, giving scholarships, building factories, increasing the productive capacity of our country, creating public beaches, converting fortresses into schools, and give the people the right to a better future—we do not endanger a single U.S. family or a single U.S. citizen.

U.S. Refusal to Negotiate

Recently, our government issued a statement that we were willing to negotiate. Why? Because we are afraid? No! We are convinced that they fear the revolution more than we fear them. They have a mentality that does not permit them to sleep when they know that there is a revolution nearby.

Fear? No one has fear here. The people who struggle for their liberty are never frightened. The frightened ones are the wealthy. The ones who have been wealthy. We are not interested in having imperialism commit suicide at our expense. They do not care about the death of Negroes, Puerto Ricans, or Americans. But we do care about every Cuban life. We are interested in peace.

We are ready to negotiate. They say that economic conditions can be discussed, but no communism. Well, where did they get the idea we would discuss that? We would discuss economic problems. But we are not even ready to admit that these talks so much as brush a petal of a rose here. The Cuban people are capable of establishing the regime they want there. We have never been thought of the possibility of discussing our regime. We will discuss only things that will not affect our sovereignty. We do want to negotiate on behalf of peace.

Those who do not worry about taking American people to war are being led by emotions. We have no fear. If they think so, let them get over that idea. No Cuban is afraid. If they think we will discuss internal politics, let them forget that, for one will do that here. Let them discuss all topics they want to discuss. We discussed things with invaders, did we not? Well, we will debate with anyone. We are willing to talk. We are willing to debate. But does that mean we are aching to negotiate? Of course, not. We are just taking a sensible step. Does that mean the revolution will slow down? Of course, not! We will continue, picking up speed as we can.

BIBLIOGRAPHY

Speech Excerpts:

October 16, 1953: History Will Absolve Me
   Castro, Fidel. "History Will Absolve Me." Spoken, Santiago
   de Cuba, October 16, 1953. Castro Internet Archive.
   https://www.marxists.org/history/cuba/archive/cas-
   tro/1953/10/16.htm]

September 26, 1960: To the U.N. General Assembly:
Cuba's Revolutionary Policy
   Castro, Fidel. "To the U.N. General Assembly: The Problem
   of Cuba and Its Revolutionary Policy." Speech, Washington,
   DC, September 26, 1960. Castro Internet Archive.
   https://www.marxists.org/history/cuba/archive/cas-
   tro/1960/09/26.htm

May 1, 1961: May Day Celebration: Cuba is a Socialist Nation
   Castro, Fidel. "To the U.N. General Assembly: The Problem
   of Cuba and Its Revolutionary Policy." Speech, Washington,
   DC, September 26, 1960. Castro Internet Archive.
   https://www.marxists.org/history/cuba/archive/cas-
   tro/1960/09/26.htm

Books

Castro, Fidel. *Fidel Castro: My Life.* Scribner. January 2008.

Castro, Fidel. *History Will Absolve Me.* Editorial de Ciencias Sociales. La Habana, Cuba. 1975.

Castro, Fidel. *The Prison Letters of Fidel Castro* Apr 29, 2009. Nation Books. (February 9, 2007)

Walsh, Daniel C. *An Air War with Cuba: The United States Radio Campaign Against Castro.* Mcfarland. October 2011.

Periodicals/World Wide Web

"A revolution is not a bed of roses": Fidel Castro in his own words. Chris Johnston. The Guardian. November 26, 2016.

"Brother Obama." Fidel Castro Ruz. Granma. March 28, 2016.

"Castro calls Jeb 'the fat little brother in Florida.'" Free Williamsburg. December 6, 2005.

"Castro: GOP primary a 'competition of idiocy and ignorance.'" USA Today News. 1/25/12

"Cuba Meeting Between Obama and Castro Exposes Old Grievances." Julie Hirschfled Davis and Damian Cave. Nytimes.com. March 21, 2016.

"Fidel Castro: Interview." Playboy. January 1967.

"Fidel Castro Announces Retirement." Truthout.com. February 19, 2008.

"Fidel Castro Quotes: Things Cuban Revolutionary Said During His 50-Year Political Life." Vishakha Sonawane. International Business Times. 11/26/16.

"Fidel Castro Dies: 23 Quotes By Cuba's Revolutionary Leader." Latin Times. November 26, 2016.

"Fidel Castro says Clinton 'discredited' Trump in first debate two weeks ago." F. World. October 10, 2016.

"Fidel Castro says his comment on Cuban model was misunderstood." Shasta Darlington, CNN. September 10, 2010.

"Former Cuban leader Fidel Castro dies at age 90." FoxNews.com. November 26, 2016.

"Hi, Fidel, this is Vicente could I ask a favor of you?" Compiled and translated by Achy Obejas. Chicago Tribune. May 02, 2002.

"How Venezuela's Military Saved Democracy (For Its Own Reasons)." Itxu Díaz. The Daily Beast. 12.17.15

"Millennials Can't Understand Castro Without Acknowledging His Legacy of Brutality." Brittany Hunter. Generation Opportunity Institute. November 29, 2016.

"Part 2 of Castro Meeting With Evangelicals." Havana Cuba Vision Network. April 11, 1990.